# Opening My Heart to God

## Inspirational Poetry and Prose

**Brenda A. Kemper Purdy**

World rights reserved. This book or any portion thereof may not be copied or reproduced in any form or manner whatever, except as provided by law, without the written permission of the publisher, except by a reviewer who may quote brief passages in a review.

The author assumes full responsibility for the accuracy of all facts and quotations as cited in this book. The opinions expressed in this book are the author's personal views and interpretations, and do not necessarily reflect those of the publisher.

This book is provided with the understanding that the publisher is not engaged in giving spiritual, legal, medical, or other professional advice. If authoritative advice is needed, the reader should seek the counsel of a competent professional.

Copyright© 2021 Brenda A. Kemper Purdy
Copyright© 2021 TEACH Services, Inc.
ISBN-13: 978-1-4796-1174-4 (Paperback)
ISBN-13: 978-1-4796-1175-1 (ePub)
Library of Congress Control Number: 2021907318

Unless otherwise noted, all Scriptures are from the King James Version, public domain.

NKJV indicates scripture taken from the New King James Version®. Copyright © 1982 by Thomas Nelson. Used by permission. All rights reserved.

# *Dedication & Acknowledgments*

There are many persons whom I would like to personally thank for their efforts in helping me realize my lifelong dream of an inspirational poetry book.

First, and foremost, is the Lord God of Abraham, Isaac, and Jacob!!! Without His Divine guidance and interposition, none of these words would have flowed from my pen to bless and encourage myself and others! I thank God, praise Him, too, for what He's done and is doing, and will continue to do with me, especially to help me accomplish my dreams!

Second, I would like to thank my beloved husband, Leslie Reed Purdy, of forty-four plus years for allowing me the joy of composing at odd hours of the day and night, while supporting me financially, cooking, washing, and spending countless hours doing various household chores for me over the years in sickness, and in health, so I would be able to enjoy being a homemaker instead of necessitating a career in nursing!! He has also helped me collect my poetry to prepare for the book, and has allowed me time to finish it sacrificing his own desires and goals that I might achieve mine!! He has brought so much happiness to my heart and our home! Truly without Les, I would not be the person I am today.

Third, I would like to thank my beloved parents, Elder and Mrs. Paul W. Kemper (Vivian) now both deceased, for their wonderful, Christian upbringing, and instilling in me the "how" and "why" to love Jesus, and for modeling the Christian life so well, that to this day everywhere I go, people tell me how much they loved my mom and dad for their genuine love for others! My minister's family with an older sister, Gwen Forrester, and a younger brother, Ed Kemper, has truly been a delight to grow up in.

Fourth, I would like to thank every single one of the prayer warriors, including family and friends, along with all the Prayer Team members from various churches who have kept my project bathed in prayer as well. Without God's direct intervention, this book would not be possible!

And last, but not least, I would like to thank my Advisor, Timothy Hullquist, and the personnel at TEACH Services for not giving up on me, and for praying me through the challenges of preparing the manuscript! Many thanks go to Rebecca, Alison, Alyssa, Bill, Karen, and the entire TEACH Services Team for their expertise as well.

It is my prayer that you will be richly blessed reading this book of devotional prayers in poetry and prose, and be drawn closer to Jesus so that you will come to know a more full and complete knowledge of God and His wonderful love, infinite wisdom, and understanding for you, the reader, His dear child!

**Enjoy!**

**Brenda A. Kemper Purdy**

*Brenda A. Kemper Purdy*

# *Table of Contents*

Wake-up Prayer . . . . . . . . . . . . . . . . . . . . . . . . . . . . . 13
By His Hand. . . . . . . . . . . . . . . . . . . . . . . . . . . . . . . . 16
Hallelujahs to My Lord and King. . . . . . . . . . . . . . . . 19
The Bible Is the Book for Me! . . . . . . . . . . . . . . . . . . 23
Old-fashioned Days . . . . . . . . . . . . . . . . . . . . . . . . . . 25
God's Rainy Season . . . . . . . . . . . . . . . . . . . . . . . . . . 31
I'll Stay with Jesus . . . . . . . . . . . . . . . . . . . . . . . . . . . 33
The Journey Ahead. . . . . . . . . . . . . . . . . . . . . . . . . . . 34
These Tears in My Eyes . . . . . . . . . . . . . . . . . . . . . . . 36
Safe in the Arms of Jesus . . . . . . . . . . . . . . . . . . . . . . 40
The Sabbath Gift . . . . . . . . . . . . . . . . . . . . . . . . . . . . 42
The Soldier—. . . . . . . . . . . . . . . . . . . . . . . . . . . . . . . 44
Ask for Big Things! . . . . . . . . . . . . . . . . . . . . . . . . . . 46
Every Morning. . . . . . . . . . . . . . . . . . . . . . . . . . . . . . 48
A Wedding Prayer. . . . . . . . . . . . . . . . . . . . . . . . . . . . 51
My Tears Are an Offering. . . . . . . . . . . . . . . . . . . . . . 52
Numbness of Sin . . . . . . . . . . . . . . . . . . . . . . . . . . . . 54
Jesus Is My Salvation! . . . . . . . . . . . . . . . . . . . . . . . . 56
Jesus Knows the Future . . . . . . . . . . . . . . . . . . . . . . . 57
A Sunday Morning Prayer . . . . . . . . . . . . . . . . . . . . . 59
Let Me Be the One Who Serves You . . . . . . . . . . . . . 61
Keep Your Eyes on Jesus, Part I. . . . . . . . . . . . . . . . . 63
Keep Your Eyes on Jesus, Part II . . . . . . . . . . . . . . . . 66
Keep Your Eyes on Jesus, Part III . . . . . . . . . . . . . . . 68
"Maze" . . . . . . . . . . . . . . . . . . . . . . . . . . . . . . . . . . . . 71
Anniversaries and Flowers. . . . . . . . . . . . . . . . . . . . . 79

*Brenda A. Kemper Purdy*

| | |
|---|---|
| Life's Journey | 81 |
| To Be Like You, God | 83 |
| A Twist | 85 |
| Speak to My Heart, O Lord, Today | 87 |
| True Beauty | 88 |
| A Prayer One Morning | 90 |
| Joy in the Morning | 93 |
| Joy in the Morning, Part II | 96 |
| Joy in the Morning, Part III | 99 |
| Today Like Thee | 101 |
| Brenda's Daily Devotions | 103 |
| Morning Devotional Prayer [1] | 105 |
| Morning Devotional Prayer [2] | 109 |
| Pre-Scripture Reading Prayer | 111 |
| Devotional Prayer from Proverbs 16 | 113 |
| Appeal | 116 |
| The Password | 117 |
| This Day | 119 |
| Biblical Counsel for a Fulfilling Marriage and a Happy Sex Life | 122 |
| The Full Day's Almanac | 125 |
| The "Mountain of Prayer" [1] | 129 |
| The "Mountain of Prayer" [2] | 133 |
| To Be Thankful-hearted as Was Sweet Carol | 137 |
| Midnight Cry | 139 |
| Morning Devotion | 141 |
| Epiphany in the Garden | 145 |
| To Be Whole Again | 148 |

*Brenda A. Kemper Purdy*

To Be Led of God . . . . . . . . . . . . . . . . . . . . . . . . . . . 152
A Song— "It Is Jesus" . . . . . . . . . . . . . . . . . . . . . . . 155
A New Mind . . . . . . . . . . . . . . . . . . . . . . . . . . . . . . . 157
No Death . . . . . . . . . . . . . . . . . . . . . . . . . . . . . . . . . . 161
My Life Just As I Am [Revised] . . . . . . . . . . . . . . . . 164
Harden Not Your Hearts! . . . . . . . . . . . . . . . . . . . . . 169
Thy Eternal Lasting Covenant . . . . . . . . . . . . . . . . . 171
The Saints Are Home at Last! . . . . . . . . . . . . . . . . . 173
Direction . . . . . . . . . . . . . . . . . . . . . . . . . . . . . . . . . . 176
Guard the Entrance . . . . . . . . . . . . . . . . . . . . . . . . . . 177
Glory Be . . . . . . . . . . . . . . . . . . . . . . . . . . . . . . . . . . 178
To Reap the Golden Harvest . . . . . . . . . . . . . . . . . . . 181
Longing for God . . . . . . . . . . . . . . . . . . . . . . . . . . . . 183
Mary's Dilemma—Our Own . . . . . . . . . . . . . . . . . . 186
A Belated Birthday Bouquet . . . . . . . . . . . . . . . . . . . 189
To a Friend . . . . . . . . . . . . . . . . . . . . . . . . . . . . . . . . 191
"Addicted" . . . . . . . . . . . . . . . . . . . . . . . . . . . . . . . . 193
Sealed into Thy Eternal Lasting Covenant . . . . . . . . 195
Dependence on the Lord . . . . . . . . . . . . . . . . . . . . . . 199
Easter Morning Revival—Will It Last? . . . . . . . . . . 203
Brenda's Personal Devotions . . . . . . . . . . . . . . . . . . 207
Inner Reflections . . . . . . . . . . . . . . . . . . . . . . . . . . . . 212
To God Be the Glory . . . . . . . . . . . . . . . . . . . . . . . . 214
To the Unsighted… . . . . . . . . . . . . . . . . . . . . . . . . . 217
Dedicated to My Blind Friends . . . . . . . . . . . . . . . . 218
Eyes That Can See . . . . . . . . . . . . . . . . . . . . . . . . . . 220
What Are You Thankful For? . . . . . . . . . . . . . . . . . . 222
Under the Shadow of the Cross . . . . . . . . . . . . . . . . 225

*Brenda A. Kemper Purdy*

| | |
|---|---|
| The Gift | 227 |
| Change Me, O God! [1] | 231 |
| Change Me, O God! [2] | 233 |
| Change Me, O God! [3] | 236 |
| Wide Open Spaces | 238 |
| THE ROAD | 241 |
| Remember | 242 |
| Judgment | 245 |
| Riley, the Cat | 249 |
| Our Friend, Arno | 252 |
| Am I Ready for Heaven? | 255 |
| Sequel to "Am I Ready for Heaven?" | 258 |
| Rebirth | 261 |
| Poem in Honor of "Miss Madison"—Our Precious Cat! | 269 |
| In Christ Alone | 274 |
| Dear Lord, I So Long to Be Perfectly Whole | 278 |
| Today's Thoughts in Prayer | 280 |
| "Baby" | 285 |
| My All for Jesus | 289 |
| God Wins Out | 291 |
| In Honor of My Beloved Husband, "Les" | 294 |
| I Surrender All | 299 |
| God's Sleep Lullaby | 303 |
| Just for Today | 306 |
| Empathy | 309 |
| God's Math | 311 |
| Expectations | 312 |

*Brenda A. Kemper Purdy*

| | |
|---|---|
| A Motto. | 314 |
| My Heartfelt Plea— | 317 |
| Trust Me | 319 |
| If I. | 322 |
| Start. Stop. Look Up and Live! | 325 |

*Brenda A. Kemper Purdy*

# Wake-up Prayer

*I woke up with these first seven lines running through my mind this early Sabbath morning August 24, 2019, so I decided to get up and write down what God gave me from about 4:30 AM to 6 AM.*

I praise You, Lord, this morning!
*Your mercies are from everlasting to everlasting!*

*I seek Your mercy—*
*I seek Your grace—*

*I seek Your kindness—*
*I seek Your face—*

*This morning, Lord!!!*

Thank You, Lord, for Your patience!
Thank You, Lord, for Your Spirit!

Thank You, Lord, for Your love!
Thank You, Lord, for Your blessings!

*(continued)*

## OPENING MY HEART TO GOD

Thank You, Lord, from here below!
Thank You, Lord, from above!

Thank You, that Your grace is enduring—
Thank You, that Your grace is truth.

Thank You, Lord, that **You so love *me!!!***
Thank You, Lord, for this very fact.

Thank You, Lord, for Your gentleness—
Thank You, Lord, I am intact.

To love You and to serve You today!—

Thank You, Lord, for the wisdom You will display—
In my life, today, Lord!

Thank You, Lord, just for being there—
The One I always can turn to—

The One to whom I pray to glorify!
Praise You, Lord, this morning!

Praise You, Lord, for being my substitute and surety—
That today, You will grace me with Your purity!

*(continued)*

And walk alongside *with* me,
To lead me to the *one eternity*!

Thank You, Lord,— this I pray—
***That I am—, becoming—, like You today!***

## The End!

# By His Hand

***Now in the morning, Lord, do I lift up my voice to Thee.
Please let my cry be heard, and listen to my earnest plea!***

**SO OFT** do I accept my fate so quick,— and unwillingly,
And oft escape the realization that no matter what might be,
One can't just do whate'er they want to achieve their goals in life,
As it seems so futile and so wrong to wait unendingly
For chance to take its mighty course, which it must do no doubt, you see!

But really now, does it come through as much as one would hope?
Does chance take over all the choices man is dealt full scope?
I do not think so, this, my friend, for in it you would find
That sooner than the cock crow twice, you might just lose your mind.
So take advice from one who's gone and traveled the journey since a time,
And learned the lessons God has taught, through His wisdom so divine.

*(continued)*

Brenda A. Kemper Purdy

One must choose to follow where Jesus goes—
Day by day, hour by hour, or even in the throes!
It is the greatest challenge in life! Trust **Him.**
*He's the One who knows*
*What is best and for our good, and for your very own good as well.*
The reader of this poem now, Take heart! He loves to come and dwell
Within the heart of anyone who lets Him slip inside—
Perhaps unnoticed by the crowd. That's alright. He doesn't mind!

So if you're listening to His voice, please look to Him today and say,
"Yes, Lord, I hear You well. I will kneel down and gently pray—
Just like I was taught so very long ago, when a small, but very young, little one
Who knew You, Lord, so well, and my journey had just begun."

Then I'll rise from my knees refreshed for the day—
To fight the good fight of faith;
For it certainly takes faith to quench the fiery darts—
And to keep the enemy at bay!

*(continued)*

*Brenda A. Kemper Purdy*

But rest assured that **VICTORY IS WON**—already at my door!
I obtained it on my knees just now, with talks to our precious Lord!
And now He will walk beside you too, to keep you in the way.
He will guide you with the apple of His eye; He will never let you stray.

So be of good cheer, my friend, the day has just begun.
The morning light is shining bright, falling down from the golden sun.
The Son of Righteousness has also arisen, and taken you **by His hand!**
With families all, let's walk on, **to the Promised Land!**

**The End**

*Written Sabbath, March 26, 2011, for my Lord and Savior, Sweet Jesus, during my devotions from about 7 to 8 AM. It was amended March 27, 2011; May 4, 2011; and June 7, 2020 also.*

# Hallelujahs to My Lord and King

*Early Morning Prayer as I Arise*

Dear Jesus, I long to be upon the sea of glass
Where I will see **You** face to face
And join the ransomed throng to sing
**Of Your** redeeming **LOVE** and matchless grace—
When I will sing to glorify **Your** name,
The music, pure and holy be—
Will lift the rafters of eternity!
I'll sound **Your** praises throughout the realm—
On eternity's doorstep just begun.
Hallelujahs to my **Lord** and **King!**

Oh, **JOY** 'twill be within my soul
Burst forth with rapturous thought and tune—
Praising God from deep within my heart,
I've last succeeded with all my part
Set forth for me from time immortal—
Praise God that at last I'll join that portal,
Of Heaven's open gates and sing—
Hallelujahs to my **Lord** and **King!**

*(continued)*

*Brenda A. Kemper Purdy*

## OPENING MY HEART TO GOD

Praise be to God— the Father, Holy Spirit, and the Son!
The Three-In-One **or** Triune God—
The hallelujahs have now begun
To wing their ways to heaven above
Where we will meet at last,
Our Author of **LOVE**!
And once more with rapturous song we'll sing
Hallelujahs to **our LORD** and **KING!**

***The End***

*Started writing September 28, 2009, about 6:50 AM. Took about twenty minutes to write, plus amending on February 19, 2014, at 1:30 AM.; and on March 15, 2014, at 5:15 AM.; finally finishing on September 8, 2019, at 5:45 AM.*

*Brenda A. Kemper Purdy*

# The Bible Is the Book for Me!

The Bible is the book for me.
Yes, the Bible is the book for me.
In its pages are rich treasures free
To help me gain eternity—
Yes, the Bible is the book for me.

God spoke of old, and the prophets wrote
Thought by thought what the Lord did quote.
Instruction to help us live each day;
Wisdom to work and teach and pray.
Yes, the Bible is the book for me.

"But," you will ask, "is the Bible true?"
"How can I be sure it will take me through?"
"Should I trust its wisdom; follow its commands?"
"What will happen should I take the Bible's way to stand?"

Listen, friend, no need to doubt;
the Bible **does** prove true!
Just follow closely the change in a life,
Which no other book can do!
Yes, the Bible is the book for me.

*(continued)*

*Brenda A. Kemper Purdy*

## OPENING MY HEART TO GOD

It's this change in a life that makes the difference
From other books to this,
For the one who heeds its counsel wins
And the rebel who doesn't, is in shame.
Yes, the Bible is the book for me.

The Bible is the book for me.
Its characters are just like you and me.
And what will work for their success
Will surely bring me happiness.
Yes, the Bible is the book for me.

**The Bible is the book for me!**

*Written before I was married, as a young adult, ~ 1971 when I completed the Master Guide requirements for Investiture Service while living in Sioux Falls, South Dakota, with my parents,*
***Elder & Mrs. Paul W. Kemper [Vivian].***

*Brenda A. Kemper Purdy*

# *Old-fashioned Days*

I took down the old family Bible today,
It's been there on the shelf for years.
The old book that holds its record
Of joys, sorrows, and tears.

*(Begin music of "Last Rose of Summer")*

Again and again I've tried to make,—
Make up my mind to look;
And tonight as I opened its pages,
A faint perfume stole from the book.

*(Last Rose of Summer)*

'Twas the smell of old-fashioned roses,
Pressed in its leaves for years.
The memories their perfume brought back to me,
Made my eyes fill with tears.

*(Home, Sweet Home)*

It took me back, back, back again,
To happy childhood days;

*(continued)*

## OPENING MY HEART TO GOD

To a dear, sweet old-fashioned garden,
Where I used to romp and play.

*(Wonderful Mother of Mine)*

And Mother,— dear old-fashioned mother,—
Sweet as her flowers blooming there!
Why, the blue in the skies was like her eyes,
The white clouds were like her hair.

*(Love's Old Sweet Song)*

The years go by, in the old-fashioned garden.
The moon shines her silvery light,
Over fragrant old-fashioned roses
Pink, yellow, and white.

*(In the Gloaming)*

And sweethearts are out there in the gloaming,
Whispering of old-fashioned love.
It seems so pure, sacred, and sweet,
God must have sanctioned it from above.

*(Spring Song)*

*(continued)*

## Old-fashioned Days

Summer has passed, the winter has gone,
And spring has come again.
Again old-fashioned roses,
Are tossed about in the wind.

*("Bridal Chorus" from Lohengrin)*

I hear the soul of an organ,
In the old-fashioned church over there,
A preacher praying God's blessings
Ever rest on the married pair.

*(Long, Long Ago)*

With an ache in my heart, and with a gentle hand,
I close the old Bible again.
To look in its pages longer,
Would bring me too much pain.

*(Last verse is read with/without music)*

I can't help but wonder somehow,
As I think of our changing ways,
If life were not sweeter and better then,—
In those wonderful, old-fashioned days!

*Brenda A. Kemper Purdy*

# OPENING MY HEART TO GOD

*Composed sometime before I was married—perhaps 1975, or early 1976.*
*(I desired the tunes [listed to the side] to be played with the verses as they were being read.)*
*Amended years later on November 13, 2014, and on Tuesday, August 13, 2019.*

# God's Rainy Season

I love the way the wind whips the trees
And howls across the windowpane.

**I think of God.**

I love to see the thick, grey clouds spread like pasted cotton
Overhead—just enough to make me wonder, is there Someone I've forgotten?

**I think of God.**

I love the rain, the constant pattering fall of water—
Lightly at times— then surely it comes in streams!

**I think of God's forgiving power.**

God's forgiving power is like the rain—
Leaving the atmosphere pure and clean, free from
Guilt and shame, and refreshing one's soul again!!

**I think of God.**

*(continued)*

*Brenda A. Kemper Purdy*

## OPENING MY HEART TO GOD

We need the rain. We cannot live without both kinds.
For with the refreshing, comes forgiveness and acceptance
**From God.**

Oh, the **joy**, of knowing God in such a close relationship
That whenever the water pours,

**I think of Him and worship!**

*Written by Brenda A. Kemper [now "Purdy"] some months before I got married—perhaps June, July, or August of 1976; amended slightly November 13, 2014; and Wednesday, August 21, 2019.*

# I'll Stay with Jesus

Jesus, I cannot somehow leave You.
For all my life I've known and learned
That You, dear Friend, are precious to me!
Indispensable for sure!
Someone I remember learning about from childhood
And wanting to do all I could for You.

Well, Jesus,—as I've grown older,—
I've had my ups and downs.
I've had opportunity to choose other ways of living—
But I've found that without You,
I am alone.

*Not even loved ones can bring complete peace.*

So stay with me, Jesus!
With You I am secure—
And what's more—
I am at peace in my soul,
So that I can be at peace with others, too.
**Yes, I'll stay with Jesus!**

**Possibly written sometime in 1978.**

*Brenda A. Kemper Purdy*

# The Journey Ahead

When all is black and grey in sight,
Oh what pain, what endless night!
I must hang on to Jesus, Precious Light!
He'll count my weakest effort right!!

He knows the wounding of my heart;
He feels the anxious, hurting loss.
He sympathizes with each welling tear;
He counts my pain as His own cross to bear!

Christ gently reminds me, "Please rest, My child,
In My outstretched arms of love and grace.
It is for you, that I have paid the price!
Choose Me always, My little one!

"And trust Me only to see you home!
Oh yes, 'tis a rough journey yet ahead, it's true,
But be patient with Me, I will escort you through
To My kingdom by My Word, with a
**'Thus saith the Lord'**!

"Remember My Word is truth, and My burden is light;

*(continued)*

Brenda A. Kemper Purdy

# The Journey Ahead

My peace I leave with you, along with the joys of doing right!
Sooner than you know, I will return and reveal
**All** the dark places, and the *'whys'* of how I cared for you so well!

"Then please take caution My child, and trust where I've gone;
The last length of the journey, I'll walk with you alone.
And help you to look above the stormy clouds that blow,
To climb Jacob's ladder and reach the highest rung—

"Of the journey ahead with Me as your leader.
No need to falter, no need to hide!
I'll walk alongside you to encourage, protect, and guide.
So that the journey ahead will be well traveled,—***with The Lord right alongside***!"

### The End

*This poem is dedicated to Lois, and all Christians on the journey to the Heavenly Kingdom. Finished September 8, 1979. Begun approximately a couple months earlier.*

Brenda A. Kemper Purdy

# These Tears in My Eyes

Why don't you wipe my tears away now, Lord?
Why do You humble me so?
I've oft' been embarrassed to speak of Your name.
Because **my** tears so easily well up and flow.

Why don't You wipe my tears away now, Lord?
So others would not see
The tears with which I freely cry,
And which You've given to me.

I cry because I love You, Lord,
And simply just for joy.
I tear because You keep Your Word
Which I really do employ.

Why don't You wipe my tears away now, Lord?
You know my heart, it's true.
But just "how" and "why" Your love I may show
Is for me to wait and lean upon **<u>You.</u>**

Why don't You wipe my tears away now, Lord?
You made me like I am, I know
With a sensitive tenderness toward Your heart

*(continued)*

*Brenda A. Kemper Purdy*

These Tears in My Eyes

    To be influenced by the Lamb to grow.

With God-fearing parents and prenatal care
    Helping to create me to a degree—
Much prayer and tenderness molding me, too,
    So I was well on my way indeed.

Oh, why don't You wipe my tears away now, Lord?
    What difference would it make?
You promised to do this when You'd come again,
    But why so long a wait?

Why don't You wipe my tears away now, Lord?
    Do You want people to feel and see
The joy in Jesus' face and life,
    Reflected tearfully in me?

Why don't You wipe my tears away now, Lord?
Precious Savior, Prince of Peace, my Best Friend!
You promised to do this someday, I'll agree.
    Won't You please do it now for me**?**

"The tears serve a purpose child! Hush! Don't complain!
Remember I made you and I still remain!
I won't wipe your tears away just now—

*(continued)*

## OPENING MY HEART TO GOD

For they serve an ultimate goal to obtain."

Salvation comes at a great price!
**<u>Jesus gave us His all—</u>**
Heaven will be infinitely worth more
Than this terrestrial ball.

Oh God,—Why didn't You wipe my tears away when
The going got hard and rough?
But still You helped me come through the fires
In spite of the trials so tough!

The water that gushed from Jesus' own side
When hanging on **Calvary's Tree—**
It reminded me of, my very own pride,
And the tears that embarrass me.

Oh yes! My Lord! You certainly desire
My response to the Spirit's call—
Then great tears well up, and often fall
To simply express my love for Thee!

For You see, dear Lord, I long to be
The person You created **me!**
And if that means producing **tears—**
And someone sees *these tears in my eyes*

*(continued)*

***With the love of Jesus reflected,—***
Then it will have been worth all the **humble years**
Of my journey of tears perfected.
For the price of a soul is true <u>**humility**</u>—
And that one soul may just be <u>**me!**</u>

Oh Lord, please don't wipe my tears away now.
Your will, I want to be done.
So I'll wait until that <u>**Magnificent Morn,**</u>
When I shall behold <u>**the Son!**</u>

Then God, Himself, shall wipe <u>**these tears in my eyes**</u>
away!
Won't that be a grand, glorious, happy <u>**Day?!!!**</u>

*(Taken from Revelation 7:17; 21:4;
and Isaiah 25:8 & 9.)*

## The End

*Written from October 2003, to February 2004, while happily living in Napa, CA, with my husband, Les, of twenty-seven plus gracious years at the time of this writing. I do not regret choosing to simply be a homemaker as a career, instead of nursing, one iota! I credit this poem for encouraging me to write a book of poetry someday. We praise the Lord!!!*

*Brenda A. Kemper Purdy*

# Safe in the Arms of Jesus

*Dedicated to Grandma Kemper & her oldest grandson [going to be deployed overseas at the time] and his wife.*

Safe in the arms of Jesus,
Safe with His nail-pierced hands.
Safe from the tempest so vivid
Pulling me down to sinking sands!

When dangers arise and hard winds fight,
Then I look up, to where I last saw the light.
When all else is hopeless, I see the faint sight
Of Jesus—the Way, the Truth, and the Life.

So I reach out and touch Him, and invite Him in.
Oh won't you do the same, my friend?
He brought me up out of a miry pit
And placed my feet upon the solid rock.

Safe and secure I shall ever be,
Safe in the arms of Jesus—eternally.

*(continued)*

*Brenda A. Kemper Purdy*

## Safe in the Arms of Jesus

Safe in the arms of Jesus,
When we obey His will and do it.—

Where Satan cannot reach us
To tempt us to stray or misconstrue it.
Safe in the arms of Jesus.
Safe I long to be—

Where daily struggles are **victorious!!!**

**Won't safe in the arms of Jesus be glorious?!!!!**

*Written in an email on October 30, 2004; Tweaked a bit on September 8, 2019. I wanted to encourage them with the protection that only Jesus could give; and made an invitation for all to let Jesus fully come in!*

*Brenda A. Kemper Purdy*

# The Sabbath Gift

*Dedicated to my own walk with the Lord—that I may always appreciate the Sabbath gift for what it was, and is, and will continue to be throughout eternity!*

Thank You, Lord Jesus, for having Your way in my heart
**For a delightful, joy-filled day.**
A day that's meant to be so very special from the start
That **the Sabbath** is its given name.

**The Sabbath**, one of God's gifts to my heart.
**The Sabbath gift** is so unique, you see.
It's like counting one, two, three …
'Cause on the seventh day, **God rested**

From all His creation—including man—
Then **blessed, sanctified**, or **set it apart**
Especially for my very own heart.
Wow! What an awesome thought!

That the Creator of the universe would set apart
*A day to be with me to fellowship, bless me,*
*And make me a chosen, unique vessel of His—*

*(continued)*

The Sabbath Gift

To encourage freedom, freedom of choice, freedom to come

To know Jesus in a deeper and fuller way;
Freedom to rest from our weekly labors, worries, guilt, and fears.
Freedom to worship God on the day He rested and made—not tradition's day.
Oh joy! My soul is full! **The Sabbath gift** precedes the gift of God's own dear Son.

What will you do to respond to **the Sabbath gift** this Christmas season?
Will you turn away from the Christ Child—your Creator-God, **or**
Will you accept **the seventh-day Sabbath** as **being the only Bible Sabbath**
That Jesus wants us to obey today?

**The choice is clear.**

**Choose <u>the Sabbath gift</u>.**

<u>**It's the best gift of all.**</u>

*Written in an email sent to my family members on October 30, 2004. I finished composing about 10:50 PM.*

*Brenda A. Kemper Purdy*

# *The Soldier—*

*Written and finished about 3:15 PM on December 26, 2004, in honor of my dad, Elder Paul W. Kemper, who later fell "asleep in Jesus" on his 97th Birthday, August 30, 2017.*

There once was a **soldier,**
**An old-fashioned soldier was he.**
He believed in high principles of his King
That would truly set a man free.

His territory was assigned,
A covert mission to be.
He left the palace of his King
To make the desired sacrifice.

Now the **soldier** went to battle.
A raging war it was.
So cruel are the weapons of destruction,
That he almost gives up hope.

But the principles of his King stand him fast;
These precious beliefs he has held to his heart so dear.
He has learned them as a little lad,
And it's brought peace and forgiveness to bear.

*(continued)*

The Soldier—

> For oft' in the dugout when enemies gun
> Bullets fly close to his head and cry, "Blood!"
> **The soldier** remembers the King's special charge:
> "Fear not! I'll send troops and power to **WIN!**"

> One battle is over now,
> But still more are ahead.
> So glad that **the soldier** knows the **King**—
> The highest commander as Friend!

The King has ordered **the soldier** back to His palace,
For his covert mission continues there.
It won't be long till all will be brought to light—
The obedience to the King, the foresight, and the excellence of **the soldier.**

The King, you see, is the Savior, Lord of all mankind!
And **the soldier** is, my Daddy dear, this wonderful Daddy of mine!

*Elder Paul W. Kemper gave God over forty years of his life as a "Servant of the Lord" in the Seventh-day Adventist Church.*

*Brenda A. Kemper Purdy*

# Ask for Big Things!

*Written on Sunday, January 30, 2005. I had gotten up early, about 4:30 AM, to the bathroom, then read and studied some. I got the idea for a poem from Matthew 7:7, and wrote this prose about 6:45 AM. Then I did a word study on "ask" in Strong's Exhaustive Concordance.*

I ask for big things from You, Lord, today.
Not just the daily answers to my often-said prayers.
I ask for a quadruple portion of Your Holy Spirit
And constant victory over self, I pray.

**Please do a *"heart bypass"* if You will—**

Specifically, Lord, I ask right now for:
Efficiency
Organization
Energy
Alertness
Ability
Calmness

*(continued)*

Brenda A. Kemper Purdy

Ask for Big Things!

Dispatch [especially great accomplishment (sky's the limit in God's eyes)]
Clarity of thinking
Keenness of memory
Patience with myself, and Les, and others
Peace that passeth all understanding
And forgiveness when I falter.
For I have an advocate, Jesus Christ, the righteous!!!
PTL!!!

Taken from:

Matthew 7:7, "Ask, and it shall be given you; …"

Matthew 21:22, "Whatsoever ye shall ask in prayer, believing, ye shall receive."

Luke 11:9, "Ask, and it shall be given you; …"

Luke 11:13 NKJV, "…Holy Spirit to those who ask Him!"

John 14:13, "And whatsoever ye shall ask in my name, that will I do, that the Father may be glorified in the Son."

# Every Morning

*Dedicated to my dear mother, Mrs. Vivian W. Kemper, by her middle daughter, Brenda, on Friday AM, February 25, 2005 before she passed away of Lou Gehrig's Disease [Amyotrophic Lateral Sclerosis] on April 11, 2005. This poem is about my having a devotional life with the Lord God, which my mom especially experienced, and I wanted to emulate.*

Every morning God's grace is new.
Every morning His tender mercies renew.
Every morning I am starting over with You, Heavenly Father.
What peace, what joy, knowing these truths.

Every morning You routinely wake me on time. (I set my alarm so as not to presume.)
And every morning You supply me strength to meditate on You, God.
Then You feed my soul as I study Your Word,
And I feed my body the good food, pure water, needed medicine You so lovingly provide.

Every morning You make me realize the value of the Master Physician,

*(continued)*

Every Morning

How You have given mankind minds to reason—
And the value of the field of medicine even today.
Every morning my study hours with You, Lord, are
more precious in every way!

Every morning now, I praise You;
Every morning now, my place is beside You.
Every morning now, I am grateful to You;
Every morning now, I am learning from You.

Every morning now, I am looking toward the dawning
Of that grand and glorious Day!
I can hardly wait the soon arrival
Of the King of Kings and Lord of every morning!
Thank You, Jesus!
PTL!

*On the card, I had also written: "Casting all your care upon him; for he careth for you" (1 Peter 5:7), and, "Thy word is a lamp unto my feet, and a light unto my path" (Ps. 119:105). And, "I'm so thankful, Mom, that you and Daddy raised us kids to know and love Jesus and the Bible from day one! Even in the womb, I will always appreciate the serious sensitivity with which you lived your pregnancy, knowing the high privilege, honor, and duties of motherhood to rear a child in the ways of the Lord. I will be eternally grateful. Love, Brenda Annette Purdy."*

# A Wedding Prayer

May the wedding bells ring out today
Of peace, happiness, and glee.
May each moment of the day,
Be filled with tributes to harmony.

Marriage comes from uniting two
Individual hearts to become one!
And what God hath joined together now,
Let not man put asunder or make undone!

And may the blessed couple know
That only with Jesus can their love grow.
For through the tests of years of time—
Will come the treasure of *love divine*.

***Written for a young couple's wedding in our church family—possibly June, 2005.***

*Brenda A. Kemper Purdy*

## *My Tears Are an Offering*

My tears are an offering to you, O God.
Freely they flow for You.
Please accept of my gratitude and praise
For lifting me from this penetrating haze—

Haze of sorrow and remorse for my sins
That caused the dear Savior's nails to be placed
Within His strong, loving, and caring hands
To pay the price sin's penalty demands.

My tears flow down for You, O God.
How full and freely they fall.
My tears are an offering to you, O God,—
What more can I bring than myself, my all?

How grateful I am, You understand,—
My beloved, my Savior, my Friend—
The way I shower You with teardrops of love!
For at these opportune times, **You** prove,

To be so very close in thought and heart!
Then my tears are a language that can start—
The process of responding to Your gracious call
To fall and kneel at the foot of the cross so tall.

*(continued)*

*Brenda A. Kemper Purdy*

My Tears Are an Offering

My tears are an offering to You, O God!
Freely they flow for You.
Please accept of my gratitude and praise—
For lifting me up from this deep, dark haze—

Into the peace that passes understanding,
And the land where there'll be no more tears!
Until then, my tears will never cease to be an offering—
Of gratitude and praise—for lifting me up from this
dark world's haze!

*Written July 19, 2005, about 4:15 PM.*

Brenda A. Kemper Purdy

# NUMBNESS OF SIN

Do you travel down the path of life with concern at sudden numbness?
Of one side right or one side left without knowledge of the purpose?
Could it be that even now, my friend, your body is approaching—
A crossroads for your life to make your life worth the living?

The choice is clear—turn around or die;
Things need to stop and change.
What could be clearer now, my friend?
The status quo no longer remains in mercy's precious train.

The numbness of sin should bring you home.
It may be your final warning chance before judgments fall,
Simply because you did not heed the Master's original call.
But do not despair. The Savior is near.

*(continued)*

Numbness of Sin

For when childlike in faith you will pray,
He always bends low to listen and lift; then gives you
the victory each day.
Praise the Lord!
By God's grace, I promise to follow God's way.

***Written August 30, 2005.***

# Jesus Is My Salvation!

He is my all in all!
He forgives my sin
And covers it with His blood
Never more to be recalled!
Oh what a sublime joy and knowledge!
What rapturous tongue can tell!
My Lord and Savior reigns supreme—
And lives to tell the tale!

*Written September 27, 2005.*
*(Pulled from another poem I had written entitled*
*"Thoughts".)*

# *Jesus Knows the Future*

**You don't know the future, but Jesus does,**
Why things happen just the way they do.
But Jesus, precious Jesus knows the future
And keeps in mind the very best for you.

Sometimes the way is perplexing, my friend,
At others, a harsh, lonely, or hurtful road.
But always, always, we can know
Jesus walks with us and saves with His blood.

Yes, Jesus **does** know the future, my friend.
For He's allowed time to fulfill prophecy,—
And He really ***does*** know the beginning from the end
When the good versus bad will be shown to win.

So it remains with us not to question—
The guiding of His hand in our past,
And to place our trust in His presence with us
In everything now, and **all** to be done that will last.

Oh, yes, we sin, and make the wrong turns,
But so has the human race, except Christ.
And when we realize this fact—
It's not so tough to bear the trials that await us.

*(continued)*

*Brenda A. Kemper Purdy*

## OPENING MY HEART TO GOD

They've been **"Master Tailor-made"** to create
The most beautiful, intricate, fabric woven—
To reflect Jesus' face with <u>**your**</u> perfect individuality;
Christ making the tapestry complete with **His** beauty!

He's coming back again very soon, my children.
And if He did not care for you and me so very much,
He would not have left behind the promises so freely given,
To teach us the lessons that prepare us to be ready for heaven!

Yes, we don't know the future, but <u>**Jesus does!**</u>
Oh, glorious thought! Jesus—our very Best Friend!
He'll make no end of joy and bliss,
When we trust to His leading for constant peace!

***And what He sees He'll make right one day—***
***As we follow the path of <u>trust and obey</u>.***
**For the Lord of the future will make life work out best—**
<u>**When we love Him and accept,—His infinite wisdom and grace!**</u>

*[Taken from Romans 8:28, one of my favorite Bible texts.]*
*Written sometime in October–November of 2002–2005,*
*for a friend's sister. Modified on February 16, 2014.*

*Brenda A. Kemper Purdy*

# *A Sunday Morning Prayer*

I want you to know, Lord, today—
That I'm a servant of Yours, I pray.
Baptize me anew with Your Spirit today.
Give me Your Holy Spirit, I pray
That I may be filled!
You choose the gifts that I need to impart
And use for others or one waiting heart.
Oh, Jesus, my Precious One,
Savior—Lord—and Best Friend—
How wonderful are Your ways—
And that without end!
Please help me today fulfill Your way
For my path of life You have planned.

My whole life's desire is in Your hand—
I'm curious, Lord—You know me—
What gifts do You have in store to give?
I'd kinda like to know,
So I can help plan the day—
I perceive I need particular ones to be sure,
But maybe, just maybe—
You've chosen other traits to procure—

*(continued)*

## OPENING MY HEART TO GOD

So, Lord— all I ask is that You lead.
I've acknowledged You, Lord, now!
Help me proceed.
I know it will not be easy—
For the road to the kingdom is narrow.

But Lord, I'm so glad that You watch me —
like the little sparrow!
You control the mighty sea.
I truly know, dear Jesus,
As You've led and taught me in my past,
You live to guide and teach me now!
I praise You for this fact!
For this is true. I have lived this truth!
I have seen it with my eyes!
I am an eyewitness like the disciples and apostles, if You will,
Of Your Spirit, and of You, sweet Jesus!
I can hardly wait to start my day with You right beside me.
Thank You, sweet Jesus! Thank You!
I love You!
Bren

*Written December 11, 2005, eight months after Mom Kemper died.*

# LET ME BE THE ONE WHO SERVES YOU

**Lord, let me be the one who serves You**
With nothing but a pure and holy faith
That lifts my part of life's burden
And helps bear the rest with grace.

**Lord, let me be the one who serves You**
And somehow let it be known
The glory shining from my face
Is coming down from the Father's throne.

**Lord, let me be the one who serves You**
And works so diligently
Cleaning, striving, studying each day,
Building for eternity.

**Lord, let me be the one who serves You**
With joy written all over my face,
And nothing less than purity of thought
Will finally finish the race.

**So Lord,— *please*— let me be the one who serves You!**

*(continued)*

*Brenda A. Kemper Purdy*

## OPENING MY HEART TO GOD

I want to do so, desperately!
Please, Lord, I'll do it.
Only with Your help I'll be

**The one and only servant of Yours**
That can fulfill my own destiny—
To work and cooperate with You completely
**So I can live sin-free!**

*Originally written Sunday, April 2, 2006, spending about forty minutes to compose; amended slightly on November 13, 2014; added to and finished Monday, August 26, 2019, about 10:30 PM. I spent about two hours total writing this.*

# Keep Your Eyes on Jesus, Part I

**At Christmas——Keep Your Eyes on Jesus——
For the New Year**

Now Baby Jesus was born long ago,
Yet He's relevant still today.
For Jesus paid the penalty on the cross
And has made our sins as white as snow.

In this Christmas season when thinking
of how Baby Jesus in Bethlehem grew,
Remember He used the very same methods,
Like **trust and obedience** too.

He had faith in His heavenly Father
That He would daily guide Him well—
Jesus kept His eyes on Father God,
But a difference those around could tell.

Yes, Jesus kept His eyes on His Father
Who never left His precious Son's side.
Since Jesus lived, died, and conquered the grave,
In Him we can abide.

*(continued)*

*OPENING MY HEART TO GOD*

Then we have our example—He's the author **and**
finisher of our faith.
Gives us courage and hope that will not let go.
To keep our eyes on Jesus is the greatest honor,—
Man can know!

If it were not for the birth of Jesus,
This earth would be in a bad way.
God sent Baby Jesus to save mankind
For that glorious, golden Day!

The key, then, lies in watching—
The babe now grown in heaven.
Who is interceding steadily
For the mighty duty undertaken.

As He bore our sins so graciously
While bleeding to death on a tree,
He was numbered with the wicked—that's **us**.
Oh why, —do we often reject Him so cruelly?

But thank Jesus! Praise God! **His blood!**
Will cover the darkest stain,
And make our hearts as white as snow;
Will cleanse and cause beginnings again!

**(May be considered "The End.")**

*Brenda A. Kemper Purdy*

# Keep Your Eyes on Jesus, Part I

***Written April 5, 2006; Begun about 3:30 PM; I worked intermittently to finish it by about 10:30 PM same day after prayer meeting. Later I read this at the St. Helena Seventh-day Adventist Church on December 30, 2006. It took about two hours total to compose all three parts.***

# *Keep Your Eyes on Jesus, Part II*

**Must Daily——Keep Your Eyes on Jesus**

Remember to keep your eyes on Jesus;
It's the darkest just before dawn.
While here, He too was tempted,
But nary a sin did spawn.

He met with the fiercest temptations
As alone the pathway he trod.
He used the very same weapon—
It was the Word of God.

**<u>I recall</u>** that Jesus walks with me.
He rose from the tomb set free;
He bends tenderly o'er me
And leads ever so patiently.

Each moment of the day as I trust Him
To give me what I need to survive
The last days' great delusions
And to bring my family home alive—

*(continued)*

*Brenda A. Kemper Purdy*

## Keep Your Eyes on Jesus, Part II

<u>**I take**</u> a moment to thank Him for being there
Just when I **most** needed Him!
And I praise Him for watching o'er me so carefully
And providing light for the way so dim!

<u>**I mention**</u> that He was so gracious!
And *still is*, of a truth, mightily so!
Gracious, longsuffering, and gentle—
With <u>**all**</u> of the lessons— I need to know.

**So I rest in peace and assurance,**
**Knowing Jesus is on my case,**
<u>**For He has never lost a battle—**</u>
**When I choose in Jesus to trust!!!**

**(May also be considered "The End.")**
*Written April 5 & 6, 2006.*

*Brenda A. Kemper Purdy*

# *Keep Your Eyes on Jesus, Part III*

**Must Now — Keep My Eyes on Jesus**

<u>**Yes, keeping my eyes on Jesus is a must,**</u>
<u>**To determine the victory here;**</u>
And receive ample portion for trials ahead,
Of confidence, joy, and gladness to spare.

Peace, and no fear—freedom from worrisome thought.
Patience that carries me through the night,
Love that renders pure, genuine delight.
Gentleness to calm the nervous ways—and faith to come to God.
Meekness to receive with readiness—the engrafted Holy Word.
Temperance included, against all, such a law is not.

<u>**So let's keep our eyes on Jesus, children.**</u>
No more need for tears a-fallin'.
He offers pardon and relief for us.
Let's take what's freely given.

To comfort and reassure our grief,
And to assure our pathway to heaven.

*(continued)*

Keep Your Eyes on Jesus, Part III

**<u>We'll need to keep our eyes on Him,</u>**
And learn the lessons given.

With strength for the battle now,
And hope for the future,
Let us ever run the race, patiently.
'Cause when we keep our eyes focused on Jesus,
We'll reign with Him now—and eternally!

**<u>So let us keep looking to Jesus,</u>**
The precious, only begotten Son!
Let's keep pressing victoriously upward;
Jesus, the Christ Child, **<u>will</u>** lead us home!

And at the freshness of this new year,
May each one fully purpose—
Let nothing waver or distract,
**<u>But keep your eyes on Jesus!</u>**

# The End!

*Written April 5 and 6, 2006, in honor of a friend in the St. Helena Seventh-day Adventist Church, a mother of three, whom I admired; I later read the poem for the last Sabbath of 2006, (looking forward to the year 2007) as part of Family Time.*

*Brenda A. Kemper Purdy*

# "MAZE"

When traveling to Canaan Land
One must be free indeed.
But how? You may ask,
Can one be really freed?

'Cause no way is shown to you
But dark and lonely paths
That one would hope would do
The mighty task of moving through—

Around the bend and next roadblock
To the goal of Canaan Land;
Turning left or turning right
Proceeding down the path at night—

Not knowing what's ahead.
This matter of the signposts
May help to show the way.
But what one needs is Jesus!

He will listen to you pray.
He hears the faintest cry for help
When one is headed into—

*(continued)*

## OPENING MY HEART TO GOD

The **"maze"** this life itself may be;

The end of which one can't deny
Of what you want to do in life.
But just as soon as you start out,
You fall into the pit of doubt!

So when you're headed down the road
And buck up against the pricks or goads,
Remember that God is with you now—
He loves you more than you can know.

And if no one's still accusing you,
You will progress, and then—
Remember you've nearly made it through
This **"maze"** you've tried to wend!

For in the heart one wonders—
How light got through to dark?
When all along the corridors
Were little bright, bright spots!!

***[May read this page for an ending, OR continue through entire poem.]***

Plants all blooming to perfection

*(continued)*

"Maze"

    Wherever they broken stand—
    Pain—the agony of misconception,
Strewn along the pathway to Canaan Land!


But there are glad moments when
Like the long, lost son came home—
They pierce into this mind of mine
Of sunnier days until when—


The road takes a turn
As I shift to the right—
Following hope in the darkness, you see—
Leading me on to a very small, candlelight.


A very small candle, indeed it is—
But sheds just enough light to pierce through—
To a door at the end of a hallway
Illumined and coming to view.


That leads me to wonder how can this be?
I've stumbled and fallen so many times.
It seems there's no hope for me going thus!
But alas, once more, the light shines!


Under the old, damp, dusty, door—
The light dispels the darkness.

*(continued)*

*Brenda A. Kemper Purdy*

## OPENING MY HEART TO GOD

When this old wooden door is swung open
And overwhelms me quickly like before—

I realize I need remember—
How countless times I'd seen
Bright, little lights, strewn across my pathway,
And courage from each it seemed,

No matter where I found them
To help me along with my walk!
**Take time to smell the roses now—**
So crucial to your **healing** somehow!

For if one did not take the time
To smell the flowers one is gazing upon—
One might not make it to **the end!**
So it behooves us to follow these little lights!

And take the time to pray and learn
That the Bible says, "He feedeth among the lilies."
So that we must likewise become,
Making use of the lights along the way—

To bring peace where happiness abounds.
And as one struggles on down the road,
Remember to count your blessings—

*(continued)*

"Maze"

For little lights here and there

Will help you in confessing—
That even though the way may be rough,
Steep, cold, dark, and depressing— little breaks of
strength one can find—
**<u>By taking God at His Word, and absolutely
not stressing!</u>**

**'Cause God's got this for you.**
Even though the way you have gone
Over stony paths so helpless that
You feel just completely tossed and blown!

But take courage! You're nearing home—
Where one will finish this **"maze"**—
Of life so abundantly shown!
So be careful! Don't be ashamed—

You have stumbled on so long—
Remember, **God has His perfect timing**
To rescue you from wrong!
**So don't give up! We're almost there!**

Through the storms and peaks of life
We must trust our heavenly Father

*(continued)*

To always lead us away from strife—
**And reach the door that will open**

**To abundant Eternal Life!!**

**The End**

# Epilogue

So whatever one does, please don't disdain
The path you just came from.
The Lord of glory will say to you,
**"Good job, My son! Well done!"**

And in the future, one will know
**The "maze" of life**—so precious below.
And you will find **God's Master Plan**—
Has always been **best for you just then!**

And you will see clearly the end of this **"maze"**
Was won with faith **and** works
Quickly moving down the corridors of time
Where delays did certainly lurk.

*(continued)*

"Maze"

> For then you will realize **God's Master Plan**
> Was worth whatever the cost!
> For you will be perfectly satisfied that—
> **<u>ALL has been done to seek and save the lost—</u>**
>
> **<u>In this "maze" called life!</u>**
>
> **The End!**

*Originally written August 9, 2006, and amended Thursday, November 13, 2014; Friday, August 23, 2019; Sabbath, August 24, 2019; finally finishing Sunday, August 25, 2019 at 5 AM. Total time spent in writing both poems was about twelve hours.*

Brenda A. Kemper Purdy

# *Anniversaries and Flowers*

Anniversaries come and go—
And so do flowers, don't you know?
Somehow day turns into week
And season into spring again.

But the lasting principle is always there,
If truly made that way from start.
Anniversaries are built on love—
The kind that comes straight from the heart!

And even though the times may fade—and even die,
These moments live on inside one's mind.
For is not this truly where the battle is?
To love or forget, the one so deserving to be loved?

This is the way with flowers too—
For they, the Creator has made.
Here today—gone tomorrow.
But, oh yes! What lasting impression they've made!!

So here it is. This is it.
Live for the day, and when done—

*(continued)*

# OPENING MY HEART TO GOD

Make sure your life is right with God,
Before the set of sun.

And while the cool stars cross the sky,
Praise Him—Who knows you best,
And has, is, and will work out
Your life's greatest tests.

For the greatest tests are the ones unknown,
Those unseen, unforecast, sudden, and alone!
"Well, fear not, gentle friend—
I, Christ, am with you now.

"Right now to the end of the age!"
Just one thing more—
Like flowers, life dies out.
Let us make our anniversaries count!!!

## The End

*In special remembrance of my father's wonderful friends' forty-seventh wedding anniversary. They were neighbors for nearly thirty years. It took about fifteen to twenty minutes to compose, and finished about 10:18 AM. on August 17, 2006.*

*Brenda A. Kemper Purdy*

# *Life's Journey*

Life takes each of us
On a unique path
Of discovery and choice.
And just because the landscape looks new,
It doesn't mean we've gotten lost.

Every mountain that we climb,
Every step that we take,
It is God who brings us closer to our dreams He makes come true—
When we follow Him with all our heart,
Not just a piece or only a part.

God really, really loves you and me!
He will meet our deepest need because—
We allow God to love us the way He does
For our lives to be fulfilling the plan
He had in mind when He created us.

Yes, "life" is a journey of many different paths.
But with God walking with us, we are never alone—
For we are promised help and light for the way,
When we place our trust in Him each day!

*(continued)*

*Brenda A. Kemper Purdy*

Praise God that He walks the paths with us!

**The End**

*Written June 15, 2007, at 12:45 PM; revised June 27, 2007, at 8:15 PM; amended slightly on November 13, 2014; and Sunday, June 7, 2020.*

# *To Be Like You, God*

To be like You

I must let go!

Why do I have to?

When others wound?

Jesus did before He died,

Or was lifted up upon the tree.

He must have let go of the soldier's pain

'Cause He said to His father in spite of the hurt,

Forgive them. They know not!

So I **must** forgive…

To be like You, God!!!

**The End**

*Written January 23, 2008; added to during fall of 2011.*

# A Twist

***The theme for this poem speaks of despair, leading to hope, because of Jesus.***

Rejected, alone again I bear the pain
Of heartache, tears, and broken dreams.
Endeavoring to gain
Repose in silence.

I flee to the Rock of ages who lifted me,
And cares beyond compare.
I only pray He will do what I cannot—
Take control of my life and make it right—

What it's supposed to be just now—
And for eternity.
**Thank You, God, for finishing Your work in me,**
For I am the clay and Thou art the Potter today.

Purge me with fire and try my emotions to see
If any wicked way is in me still.
Thank You, **Holy Spirit,** for making my will, Thy will.
Thank You, for Your love too!

*(continued)*

*Brenda A. Kemper Purdy*

## OPENING MY HEART TO GOD

Thank You, **Lord,** that You never, never, reject me!
Oh, how wonderful **You** are to me! **My Jesus!**
**My Precious Friend. You are altogether lovely—**
**World without end. The Alpha and Omega, the**
**Beginning and the End.**

And since You're all that to me and more—
Please grant to me life so abundant and free
That I may enjoy discipleship with **You now, Lord**
**Jesus, Holy Spirit, and God the Father —**
**And throughout all eternity!!!**

*Written 4:45 PM on April 28, 2008.*

*Brenda A. Kemper Purdy*

# Speak to My Heart, O Lord, Today

Speak to my heart, O Lord, today.
Speak to my heart, I pray.
Thy Word, O Lord, is faithful and true.
Speak to my heart that I may do—
All that You ask and want me to.

Speak to my heart, O Lord, today.
Speak to my heart, I pray.
Tell of Your mighty power and Spirit!
Speak to my heart that I may hear it;
That I might be not only a hearer of You—
But a consecrated, dedicated, faithful "doer," too!

**PLEASE** ——Speak to my heart, O Lord, I pray.
**YES,** ——Speak to my heart, O Lord, today.

*Written Monday morning, October 13, 2008, during personal devotions. I finished it at 6 AM; and poem was amended May 22, 2009 about 2:45 PM on the Preparation Day for the Sabbath.*

*Brenda A. Kemper Purdy*

# True Beauty

God says, "If you can see in the mirror—you're
beautiful!
Don't say you're ugly!
Take a look at yourself.
You have eyes—to view the world—

"You have a nose to smell, and ears to hear,
A mouth to speak, and cheeks to smile.
You are, My child, to **Me** most beautiful," God says.
"Because I made you for a purpose!"

"So take pleasure in knowing and liking yourself!
I made you special, like no one else!
Be thankful you are made the way you are—
Not Tom, not Dick, not Jane—but a special star!

"To be placed in My crown as one of My own!
You'll make it complete with **true beauty** your own.
For those who make up My gems, you see,
Are the ones who abide in My will so free.

"Their beauty comes from obedience—
And doing My pleasure still.
*(continued)*

*Brenda A. Kemper Purdy*

## True Beauty

Always they keep before them
My loving face, strengthening heart, and perfect will.

"They would rather die than wound me—
Or begin to stray apart,
Apart from My Spirit, so rich and free,
Which gives them a sparkle and glow so clearly.

"That no one can mistake the sweet, simple beauty,
Of loving Me as their Savior exudes with harmony;
And the actions of willing service of love to mankind,
Are freely given to all that are seen by them.

"This is **true beauty**—when one reflects Divine love in action!
It will show in their features and affection.
**True beauty** will result. **True beauty** is seen," God says—
**"The kind that never tires—and will reign eternally!"**

*Written November 24, 2008; amended August 5, 2011, and September 9, 2019. I was feeling down on my physical appearance. The Lord comforted me, and gave me these thoughts of encouragement expressed in poetry.*

*Brenda A. Kemper Purdy*

# *A Prayer One Morning*

I'm sorry, Lord, that I did not pray—
Earlier, to ask You first to bless me this day.
As I seek Your face and study Your Word,
And listen to Your voice to change my heart—
May I do the things You've planned.
That along the pathway I will find—
Strength for the journey and peace of mind.
Help me, Lord, to listen today, —
As I seek Your face and will to do, I pray—
The things You've planned for my pathway!

And as I go along with You
Close by my side, please let me know
Somehow that You are guiding me
Each and every moment of this day!
And with Your sentiments that You will send,
Please don't forget to mention today
That You are speaking with and blessing me,
In ways You only can imagine and see.
But deep inside I'll trust You'll find
Just what You're looking for beyond all time—

Beyond the bend of light and space,

*(continued)*

*Brenda A. Kemper Purdy*

## A Prayer One Morning

Into my heart preparing me to win the race,
Fought daily now with effort and prayer!
Please let me know that You are here—
To thank You, Lord, for all You do,
For all You will, and have done too!
Teach me now to ever be
More like You desire of me.
So I may go about my day
Fully equipped to talk and pray—

About the good things the Bible,
Your Word, has to share.
And, Lord, as You change my heart
With the still, small voice,
Help me ever keep Your ways in mind,
And my freedom of choice—
That I may use to decide
To follow where You lead me—
No matter where that is.
And each moment of this day—I know You will keep me.
Praise God!!!

***Written on Wednesday, April 15, 2009, at approximately midnight of the 15th, in Napa, California. The author was relaxing, writing on the computer her poetry from personal experience. May this glorify God and be a blessing to all, is the author's prayer.***

*Brenda A. Kemper Purdy*

# *Joy in the Morning*

**Written May 22, 2009**

Weeping endures, it seems—
For a whole night through.
What precious time, O Lord,
To spend with **You**!

I begin with a prayer in a dream
That really recalls
Life's great challenges
For me to do well.

It seems, O Lord,
I am finally accepting
Your purpose and plan for my life,
To be like **You** want me—

The person who follows the Lord
Alright,
With all her soul, all her body,
And with all her might!

*(continued)*

**Loving Jesus above all else**
Is my whole desire—
I weep that I've not done so,
For countless times prior!

I realize I've failed
My Lord and my God.
O how it wounds me—and does—
The path I have trod!

Although I've suffered
The pain of rejection—
From things that at times overwhelm my life,
*From friends, relationships, even my spouse—*

It wounds Jesus, too,
As much as me.
He feels the pain
Even greater—you see.

What intimate bonds are mine
to keep;
Jesus knows all about the pain
that we weep.

Only Christ really knows

*(continued)*

*Brenda A. Kemper Purdy*

The hurt I've been through—
That's why He truly is the ***Only
GREAT SUCCORER!***

But Jesus is whispering
Through the Spirit's Sweet
Voice—
**"Please!—Know that I LOVE YOU."**

**"You may *still* rejoice!!"**

"Yes, you have wounded Me—
But I know that because,
I've allowed you to walk this road—

"Your heart, and your life
Are becoming like gold.
And you're partaking of My **Raiment**
As I try you in ***fire!***"

***The End***

# Joy in the Morning, Part II

**Written May 22, 2009**

O yes, it's **not** pleasant—
But you *will* have results
With the required **desire**,
**Of Christlikeness in You—O Lord! Praise God!**

**Thank You, Father!**
I long to see **Your grace sooo**—
Must I **wait** till I fall asleep in You?
To see Your face, and thereby win the race??

***Please*, Lord, come back SOON!**
Come back soon! *Come back now!*
I'll be ready. Yes. I **am** ready!
***It's only by the grace You bestow and through faith in You!***
**Praise God!**

*(continued)*

*Brenda A. Kemper Purdy*

Anyway—what are **You** waiting for?
**You've waited long enough!**
**You** *could* **cut it short *now*—**
If ***You*** wanted to.
So what's the hold up?

I believe many people who *will choose **YOU** when given the choice **ARE** ready,*
**Lord**,
To see **You** come by **Your** grace and power only.

It's going to take **Your** signal *now* to cut it short—

**'Cause people could balk at the border again!**

However, ***SINCE***—You ***DO*** **give** **all people an opportunity** or **chance** to serve God and have **eternal life**, (see John 3:16–17), *and* You **ARE** fair and just (see John 5:30), ***what are you waiting for?***

**Please, Lord, cut it short, TODAY—**
LEAVE—NO ONE OUT—but *simply work a quick miracle* and ***finish the work in righteousness!*** (see Rom. 9:27, 28) **PRAISE GOD!**

**The End**

# Joy in the Morning, Part III

### Written May 22, 2009

You said the *"effectual, fervent prayer"* of one righteous man is not lost, but weighs heavily upon God's heart and throne. (see James 5:16-18). So **PLEASE,** since many of us down here are probably asking for **You** to come back, the greatest *"Joy in the Morning"* for me would be for **YOU to come back and take YOUR family home for ETERNITY.** I know and believe *You must be longing for that <u>same time!</u>*

Well, Jesus,—if—these poetry verses, prose and prayers count for anything as people read, pray, and agree, — may Jesus the Son, God the Father, and God the Holy Spirit be glorified in One! Please accept it, Lord, <u>as an offering of prayer, praise, confession, thanksgiving, and supplication with *entreaties for Divine power* to do **YOUR** all-seeing infinite *best and good will for* **ALL.**</u>

*(continued)*

OPENING MY HEART TO GOD

Thank You, Lord, for Your Son, and for our salvation;
and
For the ***"weeping"*** that ultimately brings——

## *"Joy in The Morning"!*

*(taken from Psalm 30:5)*

**The End**

***May He bless each abundantly. This is my prayer for you, the reader. I asked the Lord to give me a poem that would honor and glorify Him and yet express my personality and Christian walk with Him—Jesus answered that prayer—Praise God!!! Thank You Jesus!!!***

*I first finished these three poems at 8:45 AM immediately following personal devotions to God, King of the universe, Creator Jesus, and Holy Spirit, Three-In-ONE! Praise God!!! All honor and power and majesty belong to Him that sits upon the throne for ever and ever. Amen. Amen and Amen! Poetry and prose was amended several more times throughout the day [22$^{nd}$], and was finished typing about 5:45 PM, nearly 12 hours after I began writing it on scrap paper at 5:45 AM. PTL!!! Edited May 24, 2009; and August 17, 2011, at 8:30 PM.*

# Today Like Thee

## [Morning Prayer]

*Written June 29, 2009*

As I turn these pages
Help me find truth!
Please purge my soul
Of its deep, dark blots of sin and stain!

And then please control
My heart and life again!
For, Lord, I'm such a wretch, unclean,
Filthy—make me shine and shine.

So I become Your person
Who You want me to be.
Just like You, the Divine,
And emulate Your character traits.

So I can worthy taste
Of glory—victory sublime—
And walk in **this** kingdom with
Your arms embracing mine!

*(continued)*

## OPENING MY HEART TO GOD

Safely holding me close to Your heart,
Filling me full of Your wonderful love to impart—
So others may share in the joy I now know
Of trusting in Jesus,

As ruler of my throne here below.
Thank You, God, for saving one like me—
So miserable, wretched,— and now set free.
To think pure and holy thoughts today,

To live like You, Christ,
And become like You, Christ,
Is in every action, tossed-out word, and way—
To be who **You** want me to be—

Forever and today!
And with You become forever free
And truly face
Today like Thee!

**The End**

*I began about 9:15 AM and ended about 2:35 PM [five hours and twenty minutes] but probably wrote only about 2½ hours of that time.*

*Brenda A. Kemper Purdy*

# Brenda's Daily Devotions

**Written June 30, 2009, about 7:30 AM. It took one hour to compose. PTL!!!**

Dear Lord, I pray—today.
As I listen to Your voice anew,
I must die daily to self.
This I know I must do!

So Lord—just now—I surrender my all
To be made into Christ's likeness
With the character to not fall,
Just for today into sin again—

That will mar my record and
Cause sadness to reign
Not only in my heart—
But in Jesus' heart too!

For He knows exactly
What I'm going through!
So now I must trust Him

*(continued)*

## OPENING MY HEART TO GOD

*Though scary it may be,*

*'Cause Jesus will grant to me*
*The strength that I need!*
*To overcome self by His blood*
*So freely given to redeem man,*

*In cooperation with the Godhead,*
*I am sure to more than win!*
*So keep me close to Your Spirit, today, Lord.*
*Don't let me stray at all—*

*For I do not want to stumble again,*
*And make such a terrible fall—*
*As yesterday—Please help me today.*
*Lord—I surrender all.*

*The End*

*Brenda A. Kemper Purdy*

# *Morning Devotional Prayer [1]*

**Written Wednesday, July 8, 2009**

As I open Your Word just now, I pray,
Please wash me clean and take away
My sins and cast them into the sea
And cover them for all eternity.

And by Your grace and power—
Just now may I find
The strength and courage—
You have for my mind.

On today's journey with You
Through the dangers unknown,
May I stay close beside You
And keep You enthroned

In the center of my being,
The core of my soul,
The innermost chambers—
Of my heart to control.

*(continued)*

## OPENING MY HEART TO GOD

Yes, may all that I do now—
From this moment on,
Be just what you want, Lord,
Perfect as one.

In You I walk,
And together we'll run
The race set before me—
The goal that's begun.

We'll press toward the mark
And seek the straight path
Till this day is done,
And we're closer to Canaan,—

The land of my heritage—
Which You, Jesus, have promised,
Where the faithful will rest
In a place called heaven.

Oh, please, Lord, may there be—
**Not one member lost**
Of my dear family—
Who are Yours fully!

*(continued)*

*Brenda A. Kemper Purdy*

And friends, of course,
Acquaintances too,
Who are friends of Yours!
Nothing else will do.

So, thank You, Jesus,
For hearing this prayer;
For answering mightily
Before even it's breathed!

**The End**

# *Morning Devotional Prayer [2]*

**Written Thursday, July 9, 2009**

Now, Dear Lord, as I pray, Create in me a clean heart today.
Please give me a new slate as well, and make me efficient to do all things—
According to Thy great plan for me to bring
Into harmony my will with Yours today. — O let me nary a bad word say,

Or think an unkind thought to show—unloveliness in character.
As I truly want to empty self—Lord, please help me now feel right 'bout this.
I tend to question myself and doubt myself so much—
That I wonder if I really keep in touch

With You, Lord, as I ought to do? O yes, Lord, I know, I've failed before.
But just for today, Lord, please reassure—
My grain of mustard seed faith.
Even now I feel it beginning to grow.

*(continued)*

*Brenda A. Kemper Purdy*

*OPENING MY HEART TO GOD*

Praise God for His wonderful **grace**!
And even tho' I know I should not
Trust my own feelings for this or that—
Gracious God of the universe,

**You really DO care—You are so merciful—You are always there**
To encourage and comfort when the way gets weary
Lonely, hard, heavy or dreary—I am so thankful that
I **DO** trust You, God!
You're really awesome—thanks be to **You**, Lord!!!

**The End**

*Written during morning devotions on Thursday, July 9, 2009. I began about 5 AM, finishing about 6:05 AM this day. I also read Jeremiah 33.*

# Pre-Scripture Reading Prayer

*Finished July 16, 2009, at 7 AM before devotions as a prelude to Scripture reading. It took about fifty minutes to compose.*

I pray, dear Lord, today, that You will keep Satan at bay—
And help me follow in Your path
Which You have for me to take.
May I listen and not stray—that I may always make

Today a golden day in record—
From Your throne and life, I pray.
So in the sanctuary above, in which You now are,
The record of my account can be cleared by Your blood!

And recorded as such that I choose to walk
Close beside You today and consecrate even my talk,
To others, while I interact—along the road to Canaan.
I'll need all the help from my sisters and brothers—

*(continued)*

## OPENING MY HEART TO GOD

Who are willing to offer their experiential wisdom,
To aid me in my interpretation of life's boulders—
Strewn here, thrown there, to catch me off guard.
Oh Jesus, I pray,— keep Satan at bay,— today!

For without You I cannot continue my way!
And, Lord, please grant to me
Forgiveness from **all** my iniquities—
And the power to win the victories!

Thank You, God for hearing my prayer;
I totally yield now—to Your loving, watchful care
That will finish in me, what You started long ago.
"Not I, but Christ," is now my new motto!

**The End**

# Devotional Prayer from Proverbs 16

Dear Lord, I pray,— forgive me today.
Please, Lord, make me walk humbly
In Thy eternal way.
Help me, Father, understand
My foolish actions, thoughts, and plans
That I desire to do my own way
Without consulting Your Royal Majesty.
Hence I reap just what I sow.
Sometimes less, sometimes more
Of problems in communicating with others!

Didn't You have any of these to bother
Your sensitive spirit in days of yore?
You'd have problems, but it was *how*
You responded to your struggles back then, somehow,
That counts for today and the children of men.
Oh yes, it seems there were many struggles before
You died, rose from the tomb, and ascended to heaven!
Today the same problems have still arisen
In my heart as well as in other hearts' souls.
The same old struggles between the self

*(continued)*

*Brenda A. Kemper Purdy*

## OPENING MY HEART TO GOD

And Christ—who will have control?—
Will it be God? or will I be sold?
And let my life momentarily go—
Into the clutches of evil, death, and woe!
Oh, Lord, You will **not** let me go!

Please help me stay within Your glow
Of truth and safety of Your Word
So I can handle temptations' swords
And match the devil with the **Lord**—
**Mighty in battle—strong in the Word!**
Praise God! For the Savior and hope of new life!
In Christ we may have it, if we but confess
His name, our sins, and repent by His grace!
He will take care of all process—yes!
Past, present, and future—
With His robe of pure righteousness.

By faith in His mighty and holy name are we saved.
For Jesus has promised hope beyond earth!
He has conquered sickness, death, and has swallowed the grave,
Bringing life to His children
And their eternal home—

*(continued)*

*Brenda A. Kemper Purdy*

# Devotional Prayer from Proverbs 16

Where Jesus will reign
And we'll nevermore roam!

**The End**

*Written September 16, 2009. I began writing at 7:40 AM, and finished about 9:50 AM during my time with Jesus.*

# *Appeal*

***Devotional Thoughts Inspired from Proverbs 16***

Don't delay now…
Make Jesus your place of abiding
From all the problems one faces each day of our lives.
The list is endless!
But Jesus survives!
And we may conquer as He did as well.
Just step out in faith; try the waters and tell
How God moves the ocean, or builds you a bridge,
Or carries you over a gulf to the ridge.
Trust Him with all your mind, heart, and soul.
Let him take full control.
Then you will find pure joy and contentment,
Real peace of mind walking with Jesus each moment!
**In Christ is the answer!**
**Now today—**
**Just live it!**

**The End**

*Written September 16, 2009, after meditating on Proverbs 16 during my time with Jesus.*

# The Password

**Devotional Prayer Inspired from Proverbs 16**

So in Christ is the watchword, or password, if you will;
Nothing without Him is accomplished still!!!
So why not live for Jesus, O soul still deciding—
Don't delay now. Make Jesus your place of hiding!

**In Christ is the answer, O Joy of one's heart.**
Please trust Him completely, not only in part!
And take rest in the Sanctuary of Peace,
In and through Whom we partake,

Of the glories of victory,
And the world's lusts we now forsake.
Praise God for the miracles of forgiveness,
New birth,— growing in grace!

And daily walking with Jesus!
Without any of these gifts—
We could not see God's face!
Or reach the high standard with His abundant grace.

*(continued)*

*Brenda A. Kemper Purdy*

*OPENING MY HEART TO GOD*

So let's worship the King,
And fully trust in Christ,
'Cause He is doing the very best
For our happiness in life!

And as we do so—
Let us remember,
*Happy is the man who places his trust in Jesus forever!*
And our decisions will indicate whether

We use the **Password** of ***"Jesus Christ the Lord,"***
To be abundantly blessed—even in this life—
When we place our confidence and trust in **His Word**
That we may enter His glorious land beyond strife!

**Amen! Amen! And Amen!**

**The End**

*I began this on September 16, 2009; Part III was amended and finished Friday, September 6, 2019, about 6:15 PM.*

*Brenda A. Kemper Purdy*

# *This Day*

**Dedicated to a friend's mother and father, and all other grieving saints in the "Family of God."**

We do understand your pain, and grieve with you in your loss.
The **Day** is coming when **Jesus** will appear,
and **all** fears **He will forever toss.**
All graves will open wide **This Day**,
As the sleeping saints arise for me and for you to say—
All together now, **"Lo, this is our God, we have waited for Him,
And He will save us!"**
**Praise God that He has renewed us!**

Then we all will join the ransomed throng
To live with **Jesus** through all the days long
Till eternity begins again and again—
And ends only—, to begin again!— **O Master**,
Let us walk with **Thee**, fast close in these last hours.
And when the way gets rough and steep—
May we look up to where **You** keep
Shining down the light of **Your** love to guide us.

*(continued)*

*Brenda A. Kemper Purdy*

For **You** are still on the throne, and right here beside us!
**So precious Creator God, the One sitting on the throne,**
With power of the universe alone—
We humbly ask **You** to keep us strong,
So we can see **You** face to face,
Along with our family members who have finished their race!

And we trust **You** to keep us whole and complete;
We pray not one will be missing from our family to greet!
**Thank You, Lord for keeping Your promise!**
We now look for **This Day**—**You** said would dawn upon us.
And may we prepare others to greet You there too,
So **This Day** may be **joyful** for more than a few—
And the **Way**, the **Truth**, and the **Life**,—

Will make everything totally new!
So praise God! For **This Day** is coming real soon!
Let's make haste to be ready **morning, night, and noon,**
And keep looking to **Jesus** to carry us through—

*(continued)*

For **This Day** is **His Day** and **our Day**, too!!!
**Praaaaaaaise God!!! Amen! And Amen!
And Amen again!! PTL!!!**

**The End**

*Composed in about 1 hour keeping this friend's parents, and all grieving families in mind. I started approximately 11:35 PM on Saturday night, Sept 19, 2009, and finished about 12:35 AM, Sunday morning, September 20, 2009. I amended it about 9:40 PM September 20, 2009; and on Friday, the Preparation Day for the Sabbath, January 24, 2020, also.*

*Brenda A. Kemper Purdy*

# *Biblical Counsel for a Fulfilling Marriage and a Happy Sex Life*

*This was taken from my dear parents, Pastor and Mrs. Paul W. Kemper (Vivian), who enjoyed an abundant life for more than sixty years of wedded bliss! Praise God!!! Information gleaned from an interview with Dad on Jan. 17, 2010, (who went to sleep in Jesus on his ninety-seventh birthday, August 30, 2017. Mom died first on April 11, 2005). Both are now awaiting the Resurrection Morn not far distant. I received the information and typed it the same day—Jan. 17, 2010, with adjustments in 2020.*

The enemy can get us upset for many or any reason(s). But,— be a living example of love anyway. (Please see 1 Cor. 13.)

Enjoy sex (meaning <u>the full act of love</u> including foreplay and intercourse).

This must be what is mutually agreeable (*without pressure),* and must be relaxed and rested.

"Praise God, from Whom all blessings flow! Praise Him, all creatures here below. Praise Him above, ye heavenly host.

Praise Father, Son, and Holy Ghost." Amen.

*(continued)*

Biblical Counsel for a Fulfilling Marriage
and a Happy Sex Life

He mentioned about Romans 8:28 still being 100 percent true every time. And that God has a plan for each life that will make it an abundant one, full and free, but we must choose it to be so! It is our choice.

Let us choose to become the men and women whom God would want us to be, fully dedicated to the Lord with all our hearts, minds, bodies, and souls, and we will reap the benefits not only of eternal life in the kingdom of heaven, but also here on this earthly journey as we travel along the way.

And God still has a work for us (you and me) to do in our marriages! Choose it!
(please see Joshua 24:14, 15)

Praise God, for He is worthy to be praised!!!

*Brenda A. Kemper Purdy*

# The Full Day's Almanac

**To find God's daily will and peace, please follow the steps below:**

**1. To be in God's will**—Read Psalm 40:8, "I delight to do thy will, O my God: yea, thy law is within my heart."

**2. To be in God's will**—one must follow His lead.

**3. To be in God's will**—one must follow His lead to His ultimate hill, Golgotha (the Cross).

**4. To be in God's will**—one must follow His lead to Golgotha and beyond, until Jesus comes again.

>   **4a. To be in God's will**—one must follow His lead to Golgotha and beyond, until Jesus comes again, knowing we must first lay our plans down at Jesus' feet, and follow in His footsteps and boot prints.
>
>   **4b. To be in God's will**—one must follow His lead to Golgotha and beyond, until Jesus comes again, listening closely to His Spirit, and be willing to change our plans at any moment. (In other words, being flexible with our plans and

*(continued)*

> alert to the voice of God to the heart, mind, body, and soul are vital.)

5. Then—at the end of the day, having done God's will for your (our) life(s)—simply trust God to fill in any weakness with His strength. And He will take care of the rest! PTL!!! (Please see II Cor. 12: 9–10)

6. Trust Jesus to cover you with *His robe of white!*

7. Sleep in peace knowing you have done His will! Rest in His promise—He will not forsake you now! Go to sleep! (Please see Psalm 127:2)

### ***Written January 18, 2010.***

# THE "MOUNTAIN OF PRAYER" [1]

Everyone needs a special place
Where one can go and find release
From daily cares of toil and sorrow
And find strength to meet the morrow.

So the "mountain of prayer" becomes my haven where
I know I can retreat—
Any time of the day or night, my friend, with my four
walls to lock me in!
With one window to let in light, a bed and a pillow or
two or three,
A cozy cover and/or comforter to keep the coolness at bay.

It works for me—this "mountain"—
To search out the things of God in my heart,
And meet with the Lord to discuss my troubles—
With all the grit and grain that I've got!

But something just occurred to me—
My "mountain" has moved to include,
The "hills" in the living room area too,
Where my easy chair also resides!

Ever ready to spring its foot rest to action—
So I may rest my weary legs and feet!

*(continued)*

*Brenda A. Kemper Purdy*

## OPENING MY HEART TO GOD

Since the "mountain of prayer" has enlarged its borders,
I can talk to God in like manner sweet!

Take note, my friend, when you're now reading this.
**All** need a special "mountain of prayer" to retreat—
Be it four walls with a window, an easy chair, or Alps,
Each place serves its special purpose, you see.

And when you realize its true worth—
The "mountain of prayer" will become your lifeline
To make your time here a little heaven on earth!
For we each must obtain worthy characters—

As pure and precious as gold.
No small effort on our part 'twill take
As we live, work, and play each day!
The "mountain of prayer" will assure for you and me,

A place in that city so fair—
And make the fact become reality—
Of a holy, Christlike, character!
Praise God for "**the mountain of prayer!**"

### The End

*The Lord gave this to me out of my personal devotional experiences! It took about 1 ½ to 2 ½ hours to write. I began about 6:30 AM, and finished about 8:30 AM on September 1, 2010.*

# The "Mountain of Prayer" [2]

I've come into my "mountain,"
And my "mountain" has come to me.
The place where I can talk to God
And think so ponderingly.

The **"mountain of prayer"** within my room
Enclosed by four walls it is.
At night and in the early morning hours,
I listen to this voice of His—

His voice that speaks so tenderly,
And woos my aching heart!
The One who comforts willingly to never, e'er depart—
From being right close by my side,

To help in my time of distress!
It seems I can think, worry, cry, and talk to God,
Without any fears at best—
For I've got a private audience chamber—

With the King of kings and Ruler of the universe!

*(continued)*

*Brenda A. Kemper Purdy*

## OPENING MY HEART TO GOD

He **does** take time to notice me
When I call upon Him for service.
God seems to be a captive listener,

At these very special seasons—
When I'm in my room, alone, or with my husband—
Praying softly in my heart and mind, to You, Lord,—
Who is so kind!
Yes, the **"mountain of prayer"** has become my bedroom—

Whenever I rest my bones!
And in the early morning hours,
I seem to spend my time with You, God,— hearing your tones—
While rehearsing the whole day before—

When some things have gone tough with me.
When I've made mistakes galore!
And sinned so deeply that I regret my choices—
Even to think about things much more!!

Then somehow this "mountain" looms up—
And reaches to the very throne room above!
I have a "one-on-one" with God.

*(continued)*

## The "Mountain of Prayer" [2]

I tell Him like it is with me—

And He tells me where, why, and how to trod!
So I listen carefully, and tearfully thank Him—
For the privilege of speaking so intimately with a person like He is—
A Counselor, Friend, Lover, Confidant, and God!

Who could ask for anything more than this,
From the God Whom we all adore?
Yes, the **"mountain of prayer"** has served me well!
For great peace comes over me—such that I **am** able to tell—

In my heart of the great love that God has imparted
To soothe my troubled mind,
And the oil of the Holy Spirit smooths any hurts I've pondered—
While at this **"mountain of prayer."**

And I am refreshed and strengthened,
To begin the new day with care!
Now if,— one may say, "Why do you choose your bedroom—
Instead of a 'real' mountain to pray?"

*(continued)*

*Brenda A. Kemper Purdy*

The answer is, "I do not have access to a quiet place
like Gethsemane—
So I make the 'mountain' come to me!!!"
After all—
Nothing is impossible with God—
In His **"mountain of prayer"** you see!

*(Please see Matt. 19:26)*

***The End!***

***I wrote this on September 2, 2010, for my morning prayer.***

# *To Be Thankful-hearted as Was Sweet Carol*

To be thankful-hearted as was sweet Carol, is no small, feat!
For she constantly, graciously, thanked **all**, whom she would meet.
She lovingly gave of the gifts she adored
To those who suffered or were worse off than her.

She even gave to her friends who didn't need—
The treats she so willingly offered indeed!
Yes.— Carol was truly a thankful-hearted person!
She was a generous, and giving kind of Christian!

She will live on in the hearts of the people that knew her.
To be thankful as sweet Carol will challenge us to give the same care.
But Carol's God will help us, as He sustained her—
To be caring for others, giving them treatment ro-yal!

If we choose, we can become thankful-hearted, as was sweet Carol!

*(continued)*

*Brenda A. Kemper Purdy*

*OPENING MY HEART TO GOD*

Praise the Lord!!! And thank the Lord for the life of sweet Carol!

**The End**

*I wrote this poem honoring Carol E. Chiu, a dear friend, and read it for her memorial service on December 7th, 2010.*

# *Midnight Cry*

**Written during the middle of the night, when I could not sleep.**

I cannot sleep, Lord,— what can I do?
It seems that I'm stressed, Lord, beyond my control!
I need You more now, Lord, than ever before—
I'm pressed to ask questions of **You** in my heart—
Don't I deserve answers right now from the start?

You know, Lord, I love You, and try to delight—
In all of Your ways that make You first in my heart.
But somehow it just doesn't seem to add up!
The answers I get, don't match ones
That I want!

Why is this so, my Lord and my God?
I've tried to delight in **<u>You</u>,** Lord.— Honest, I've tried!
Why, then, don't You honor the promise You've made?
Is it because I've not fully trusted Your Word?
Or, because I'm not fully surrendered my Lord?

This really must surely be part of the fault,
'Cause nothing from Your end will ever fall short!

*(continued)*

*Brenda A. Kemper Purdy*

*OPENING MY HEART TO GOD*

So help me, Lord, to finish the task—
To delight in You fully,
And do whatever You ask.

To complete the perfect work
You've set out in me to do—
Accomplishing in me,
The building of my character—
For Your eternity!

**The End**

*This was written about 2:30 AM, on the morning of our thirty-fourth wedding anniversary, December 19, 2010. It took approximately thirty minutes to write. It was amended December 15, 2013, extremely early in the morning about three years later in the week of our thirty-seventh wedding anniversary, as well as on the evening of January 26, 2020, about 10 PM.*

*Brenda A. Kemper Purdy*

# *Morning Devotion*

**Written January 3, 2011, in honor of a wife and mother in memory of her husband, who recently was tragically killed in a car accident, leaving her two young boys, and the baby girl on the way with no father, and she without a husband.**

God,— please,— I lift up this woman and the boys to you today, and the expected one, too—may all go well with the little one on the way.
Please give her strength and courage—peace to pass the day, with some joy in her heart, knowing You only can impart
The genuine peace that passes, understanding of the heart!
Help her forgive herself and let all go of any remnants of the woe
That may tempt her to fear, worry, fret, or paralyze her, or cast doubt into her mind as yet.
May there be no room for doubt or fear, or any such thing to cast a tear.
The children really still need her loving care—
May she be all she needs to be to them in this situation here.

*(continued)*

## OPENING MY HEART TO GOD

Please, Lord, I lift her and the little family up again to You.
Watch over them today and keep them in the narrow way.
Also watch over me, I pray, as I go about my day—
Keep my tongue from saying anything
That might offend or sting or rend!
Because I am so afraid I'll stumble
And make an awful, awful big bumble
Of my day.— It seems I am so weak in so many areas,
Even as I speak, that I just, **must**—
Do my very best—
To cling to Jesus more and more,
And leave to Him the rest!
The rest of all that I know there is to gain
The victory over in my very own domain
Of life today, and each and every day
For the rest of my life in every way!
Amen—Amen—and Amen again!
Praise God! We may begin this day!

The End

*Lord—please bless my Sweetheart, Les, and his day too—his every thought, action, and move. Please watch over him, and keep him safe. Spare his life,*

*(continued)*

*please, and guide him, too. Help him realize how much I love him—and help me be able to truly make him happy. This is my prayer today. The P.S. was written on May 4, 2011.*

# *Epiphany in the Garden*

***I wrote this on Sunday, January 16, 2011, inspired by my friend (alias a church secretary) who loves gardening, and had a wonderful vegetable garden this year! My husband and I have reaped the benefits of her tasty harvest many times at church potlucks and other activities. Thank you, friend, for inspiring me to write about you spending a day in your garden!***

When the way is hard,
I go to my yard
where flowers and vegetables grow each day.
I work and toil
planting the soil
Till blisters are raised, **and I begin to pray.**
I dare no more foil
The weeds with my plans
So plants can birth and grow off the land,
**Unless I dig deep**
Down into the rocks
And pull hard and fast
To get the **roots out!**
**'Cause weeds surely do have dark roots old**
**Roots that should have been pulled out long ago!**

*(continued)*

*Brenda A. Kemper Purdy*

## OPENING MY HEART TO GOD

But be that as it may,
I am kneeling here now—
Tugging—pulling—and wiping my brow.
<u>The flowers are blooming so bright and so fair.</u>
<u>The veggies are young and most ready for fare.</u>
***<u>The garden is growing—praise God!!!</u>***
This miracle I face
Is truly from heaven
**Through divine grace!**
And as I kneel here now, Lord,
In my garden today—
<u>I just ask that **You'd take**</u>
<u>**All my sins away**</u>
<u>**And bury them deep**—deeper than the rocks—</u>
<u>Into the sea—</u>
<u>**You said You'd throw them away for me!**</u>
Yes, God, as I work in my yard today
**I've drawn closer to You,**
**And You've taught me to see—**

*To see myself for who I really am.*
Lord, You know—
**This plant can't live without**
**Your bestowal of life here below**
**And complete renewal**—so—o—oh—

*(continued)*

<u>Make me new today as You have made these plants grow.</u>
**Create in me a clean heart, O God,—right now!**
**And take not Your Holy Spirit from me.**
<u>I'll trust You for this.</u>
Please, Lord—
Take over my life!
Empty self!
Fill me with **love**—
**<u>Growing evermore like You, Christ!</u>**

Thank You and praise You—
For Who You are!
You have now done it—
**You are King by far—**
**In this garden yard!!!**

**The End!**

*This took approximately one hour and fifteen minutes to write (split up throughout the day from about 10 AM—5:30 PM).*

*Brenda A. Kemper Purdy*

# To Be Whole Again

**Written May 8, 2011—in the early morning (about 4 AM) on Mother's Day, in honor of my parents, Pastor Paul and Vivian Kemper.**

**"To be whole again!"**—This is the gift Jesus has given to me for my mom (and dad)— something that really thrills my soul to the N$^{th}$ degree!!
A gift so wonderful to uplift e'en my weary soul, traveling so swift—
That my soul is encouraged—to live—and look—and rest—and breathe!
Rest so that I may continue to trust—
The divine Son of God who makes it a must
For me to purposely do all that I desire or want,
Or even set out to do for You, Lord!

What a magnificent way to be—**whole— complete— and free indeed—**
To feel without fear, and love again myself, as God does.
Forgive myself too. O joy of loving without fear or guilt and feeling free to be myself,
And love others too, as Jesus would!

*(continued)*

*Brenda A. Kemper Purdy*

## To Be Whole Again

**"Whole again!"** The very thought sends moments of awe running to my brain
To remember when days were not so happy or plain.
And yet anyone now can say just what they think— and feel safe with each other,
That no laugh would be caught or tossed into the rink,—
Somehow by a careless smirk or a downturned brow.
O no, my friend. **"To be whole again"**—one does not experience "now"— just like before!
Than even before yesterday,— for since then I've grown in Christ a wee bit more.


And praise God! What a wonderful chore to accomplish each day in an orderly way,
And keep up with the times—to be ready to go to the sweet Canaan Land—
Where there'll be **no more brokenness,** or any **holes** to be filled!!
Won't that be grand? Just to see Jesus fill our hearts with love and take us each by the hand!
**There we will be "whole again"! Forever and forevermore to stand!**
Praise God, how He leads His children o'er!


*(continued)*

*Brenda A. Kemper Purdy*

## OPENING MY HEART TO GOD

**Now we must open the door of our hearts each day**
To let Him take all the dross away,
And then make us just like He wants us to be—
More fully reflecting God's character so free!

*We each are broken in need of the Savior—*
And someday **if** we accept Him, we'll be **perfectly favored!**
Let's all meet 'round the Tree of Life, rejoicing **then.**
No more empty, self-conscious lack, but **one solid mind— whole, and intact!**
The **JOY** of knowing that this will someday be,
**Helps offset the waiting** for time unending, don't you see?
When reality will be the dream—
**And fully satisfied we'll be———**
**Made perfectly whole by Jesus Christ, the Risen Lamb—for all eternity!**

**The End**

*I began this poem about 4 AM on May 8, 2011, and finished about 5:35 AM. I got to bed very late as Women's Ministries' Retreat was this weekend—I had a blessed time. The Holy Spirit was truly there! But I didn't sleep*

*(continued)*

*too well. This theme [To Be Whole Again] kept running through my head, so I decided to write a poem with God's help, of the joy and renewal, I experienced during the meetings. I felt connected like never before. Praise God! I truly enjoyed the time with my sisters in the Lord!!!*

*I wrote in honor of my beloved parents who had loved me through the ups and downs of experiencing a Bipolar life! I am so thankful to God for my parents' loving acceptance and encouragement in spite of the fact I was Bipolar!! I longed for the Day when I would receive a new mind, and truly be* ***"Whole Again!"***

*This was amended slightly about 6:15 AM on May 8, 2011; about 2:30 PM August 17, 2011; about 6 AM March 2, 2013; about 5 PM December 4, 2013; and finally about 6:30 AM August 23, 2019.*

*OPENING MY HEART TO GOD*

# To Be Led of God

Like a missile aimed so sharp
Ready to pounce upon its mark,
God is guiding those who trust
Implicitly in His abiding presence, thus—

One comes away with such peace and joy
Knowing Jesus has determined the route that one takes
to obey.
For one oft can get confused in life about the way to
turn—
At the crossroads of decision seems—there's always
heavy loads.

Baggage hindering the plain sight
Of better goals ahead.
So realize, friend, that Jesus cares,
There is no need to dread.

For He sees each turn we take,
And when we practice keeping Him in front,
He will not forsake.
Because He will finish what He's started—

Even though it's tough to see
How possibly, possibly in the world this can truly be?

*(continued)*

*Brenda A. Kemper Purdy*

## To Be Led of God

So rest assured now that you have done
Just what you've chosen to do.
If in fact it should be otherwise
Our precious Jesus will tell you even so!

When God is leading His dear children along
As they cooperate with **His mighty hand,**
There's nothing to worry about—**if**,— one may choose wrong.
**For in God's tender mercy, he or she can be forgiven—**
IF one comes to the **Cross**, where all may be cleansed,
And finds in Jesus—the way home again!

On the way to Christ and His white purity,
God looks down upon us with certain surety.
And as we follow His lead and allow the Spirit to guide,
We will certainly find Him abiding right inside!
Step by step does He walk along beside us,
**Leading us each,— just as He promised!**
**The End**

*The Holy Spirit gave this poem to me, and I wrote down the words on May 9, 2011. I began about 1 AM and finished about 2:05 AM. It took nearly 1 hour to compose on the theme of "God leads His dear children along". It was amended on December 27, 2012 by 12:30 AM, and again at 10 AM same day.*

*Brenda A. Kemper Purdy*

# A Song— "It Is Jesus"

It is Jesus. It is Jesus.
Come to Me, and trust in Me.
It is Jesus.
I will do for you what you cannot do.
I will make your heart pure and clean again.
I will keep your heart pure and clean today—
Just trust Me and I will make you be like Me,
And finish what I started.
O so long ago, it seems to me, but to **You**—
It's just a moment in time.
It is Jesus. It is Jesus.
I will care for you. So do not worry.
I will help you make it through. You'll be OK.
So Jesus—is my very Best Friend!
He will help me to the very end—I'll be safe in His arms (or hands)!
It is Jesus. It is Jesus.

**The End**

*When the night before I was concerned and afraid*
*If my husband would die,*
*And I'd be left alone till Jesus returned*

*(continued)*

*Or for anytime at all,*
*The song and melody woke me up.*
*I sang "It Is Jesus" as a morning prayer to God upon awakening about 4 AM, and wrote it down by 4:40 AM on May 10, 2011.*

# A New Mind

***Written May 26, 2011, from 3 AM to 5 AM. I had difficulty sleeping, and wanted to pour out my soul to God through poetry. I asked God to help me through prayer, and as always, He did!***

When will I have a new mind, Lord?— Oh, I long for that day!
A new mind that will work and think and be able to really stay
In focus on life, enjoy the ride—without worry or guilt or fear?
A new mind that will not be tempted to cling——
To thoughts so obtrusive they make one to shudder
At what would happen if they were uttered.

O, for a new mind ***now***, my Lord! Could that be possible?
These thoughts of mine are so messed up, it seems at times so reprehensible!
You said You don't want there to be confusion in my thoughts—
So why do I have to have such a mixed-up mind wrought?

*(continued)*

O, Lord—a new mind, I want! A new mind, I desire!
Please grant me peace!
In my inmost being I so require that You, Lord, do this,
for me—
And grant unto me a new mind so free.

So free and clean that I can smell
And taste the purity of heaven's air surrounding me!
A new mind at last—I will have some day.
*O joy, Lord!* Please keep me strong until that time, I pray!!
Faithful to do Your will.
Keep me ever growing more like You
In body, spirit, mind, and soul,
So that by beholding I may become—
One like Christ's mind, with **a new mind** in me,
dwelling as one!

**The End**

*I am happily married to Leslie Reed Purdy for over thirty-four years at the time of this writing, and living in Napa, CA; currently enjoying our "son", "Buddy", a black and white Border Collie-Australian Shepherd Mix, [given to us by our nephew and family].*

# *No Death*

*Started poem about 4 AM and finished at 5:35 AM on July 26, 2011. I wrote it in honor of our beautiful pet dog, "Buddy" (part Australian Shepherd/Border Collie Mix, with one blue eye and one dark brown or black eye, with a charcoal black, fluffy, furry coat with white trim, looking much like "Lassie" only black and white). He is approximately nine years old and is dying of seemingly kidney failure, as he is drinking profusely, with complete loss of appetite.*

*My husband and I long for the Day when Jesus comes and will put an end to sin and suffering, even to the suffering of our precious little innocent pets! Praise God! O Hasten on that glad Day when we will be able to say, "Lo, this is our God; We have waited for Him, and He will save us. …. we will be glad and rejoice in his salvation" [Isaiah 25:9]. PTL!!!*

*We were taking him to the vet that AM to have him taken out of suffering. O come sweet Jesus. We found out that Buddy had a bladder infection. He perked up for a short time [about 1 ½ months] until he was unable to walk well, and got really confused evidently from a spinal tumor also. So on September 14, 2011,*

*(continued)*

*we decided to have him put "to sleep" and out of his suffering. We believe he is resting in his grave until the Resurrection Morn. O Come, sweet Jesus!!!*

*******

O Jesus, come quickly and ease the pain of death and sorrow;
The hurt is so bad, so deep, please come to end the morrow
When there'll be **NO DEATH** of any kind,
No separation, or loss, or crying to find—
Only that one's "best friend," so to speak,
On this dreary, lonely earth
Has taken a mighty big turn for the worse.
And seemingly now, the time has come—
To part our way with a thing called **love.**
But is it really true? One may say—

Part the way with this thing called **love**?
I do not think so. As **love** is from **above!**
And once it has taken root among the soil,
It digs deep to find strength for the daily toils
Of living in a world of care,
And blessing all those it touches there.
For you see, my friend, **love** abides—
In the heart of anyone who truly resides

*(continued)*

## No Death

In the Master's hands Who so lovingly holds
The world upon its billowy folds—

And takes care of even the sparrow that falls.
For He watches o'er me and you
Till the evening sunset calls—
To end the day—. Then on in to the night—
God continues His careful watch,
With **love** from God and **love** toward men
Even **love** for the animals who travail in pain.

Someday there will be **NO DEATH**—
To make us so very sad again!
And when **THAT DAY** appears
(Which is not too far away right now),
We'll be more than happy and ecstatic with ***JOY!***

So let's keep on truckin'— for Jesus' sake! Shall we?
Let's be the first to greet our Christ
In His home so full of **love** for us—
Where **NO DEATH** will reign forever,
And death's price is paid—through all eternity!

**The End!**

*Brenda A. Kemper Purdy*

# *My Life Just As I Am [Revised]*

**My life just as I am,**
**An offering to the Lamb.**
**This is all I can bring.**
**I know no other thing.**

Lord, just now I gaze at Your feet,
I long to be Yours—whole and complete.
I don't know how or what it's like to worship **You**,
In perfection, harmony, without sinning true.

But Lord, what am I to Thee?
Am I worth all these tears before eternity?
When in my past I've messed up so
And currently am not much better yo!

Seems I haven't gotten very far in life
For the time I've traveled and spent in strife.
There've been roadblocks, hindrances, circumstances, you see—
O why, *O why*, did You make one like *me*?

*(continued)*

*Brenda A. Kemper Purdy*

# My Life Just As I Am [Revised]

(My head seems so large and eyes out of shape)
(Neurologically not normal, can You, <u>*really*</u> **relate?**)
O God, I somehow know **You** can,
And that You chose to make me part of **Your Plan.**

But I fall so short of **Your Divine Life Plan**.
I'm just sure of it, Lord!
Seems few times **The Plan** I've done.
Yet I realize without **YOU**—

The Plan I can't run!
And I wonder, "Do I really have **YOU** in my heart to begin
My life just as I am?
Covering my life—

Taking control—
Right from the start?
Making me whole?
An offering to the Lamb?

While I need to remember the way **You've** held me fast,
Through many troubled waters threatening,
And from my very unstable past!
**You've** kept me alive—and made me last!

*(continued)*

*Brenda A. Kemper Purdy*

## OPENING MY HEART TO GOD

Somehow, Lord, the thoughts do come—
Have I really surrendered completely to **You, the Son?**
As I ponder what **You've** done for me
I can't help myself but weep and weep!

O what an unworthy, unworthy, soul am I**!!!**
Yet in Your love and mercy, **You** really died—
To show the way through my treacherous sin
Just to make me truly whole again.

Your still small voice speaks to me still
And what do I hear—pray I tell?
I hear the voice of One so humble
Who gave **His life** for me—that I might not stumble.

Praise God from Whom all blessings flow!!!
And <u>**nothing**</u> does He expect from me—
No payment, no achievement,
**Nothing**—I'm free!

No working my way to eternal bliss.
Just can't do that, **for I'd totally miss!**
There's **nothing, nothing,** I can do
To make the record pure and true!

**Except trust in Jesus**

*(continued)*

*Brenda A. Kemper Purdy*

## My Life Just As I Am [Revised]

**While relying on Him**
**To give me victory**
**Over ALL my sins.**

I finally realize once again,
**That I can't do it!**
Without trusting **ALL** to Him—
**And giving my life—just as I am!**

### Epilogue

**I now live in peace following the Lamb.**
And with it comes joy from the **great I AM**—
Life so abundant, fruitful and free
Knowing Jesus has taken **ALL** my sins for me!

**And covering them with His precious "robe,"**
God can now look down upon this lost globe
Seeing Jesus only while covering me
Spotless, pure, righteous, and clean!

Yes. God sees Jesus only
Who paid the price—
For the **"robe of white,"**
Comes with great sacrifice!

*(continued)*

*Brenda A. Kemper Purdy*

*OPENING MY HEART TO GOD*

And deep inside—I trust in Jesus
Who'll give me new opportunities to fulfill
My destiny lingering in the balance still—
And my salvation made sure at the Cross.

**My life just as I am**
**An offering to the Lamb.**
**God only wanted what I have brought.**
**All He ever needs—is my surrendered heart!**

**The End**

*Composed September 24, 2011, by the inspiration of the Holy Spirit for devotions in the middle of the night (midnight to 2:30 AM). I prayed the Lord would give me a poem to express how I felt early that morning while talking to God in private devotions. He answered that prayer. It took about 2½ hours to originally write and was revised on January 16, 2013, at 5:15 PM; October 5, 2013; February 20, 2020; and June 15, 2020. The Lord is good! And we have a lot to be thankful for to say the least!! PTL!!!*

*Brenda A. Kemper Purdy*

# Harden Not Your Hearts!

Father, today, give me, I pray—
A heart like Thine with total surrender sublime.
A heart pure and clean;
A heart pure to dream.
A heart that's right to act the part of noble deeds,
And kindly start its way to heavenly kingdom come,
The everlasting home above—
For each of us to see and live
Throughout eternity.

Praise God He's made you and me
To be able to be free—
To make the choice of this precious trip
To Canaan Land you see.
Now has come the time to decide.
Will it be you, my friend, or me, or none of us—
To abide with Him? ?
Nay—I pray.

But as for me and my house—
We will serve the Lord! Won't you join us?

*(continued)*

*Brenda A. Kemper Purdy*

## OPENING MY HEART TO GOD

Praise God!
Come to the banquet He's prepared for us today!
Do not linger or wait—
But hasten to obey.
For now is the accepted time—
And day of salvation.
Won't you come to Him today? ? ?

**Harden not your hearts!**

**Follow Christ—the Truth,—the Life,—the Way!**

**The End!**

*Inspired by the Holy Spirit and God's Word on November 18, 2011, about 3:45 AM.*

# Thy Eternal Lasting Covenant

Seal me in Thy eternal lasting covenant—
Seal me in Thy eternal lasting way—
Seal me in Thy eternal lasting moment—
Only for Thy eternal lasting day!

Lord, keep me sealed to Thee eternally—
Under Your wings let me abide—
Let me press close into Your garment—
And take sweet rest by Your ever-pierced and wounded side.

The water from Calvary refreshes me—
Like no other I've ever known!
O Savior dear, please hold me
Close to Your abiding throne.

I know I'll need to rest now,
Perhaps lay my heavy burdens down.
But soon I'll hear Your clarion call
When You reach to give me my crown.

*(continued)*

*Brenda A. Kemper Purdy*

*OPENING MY HEART TO GOD*

You'll say, "Well done, My child—
You're sealed at last—
Into My eternal lasting covenant!
Welcome home forever!

"I can trust you now to be victorious—as My Son—,
the living Christ!"

**THE END**

*Inspired by devotions on 1 Corinthians 12 and 13 on February 14, 2012. Begun about 4:30 AM and finished about 5:30 AM.*

*Brenda A. Kemper Purdy*

# The Saints Are Home at Last!

***Written for devotions on February 14, 2012***

Please, Lord, as I linger—
Near Your throne so full of love,
Let me but catch a glimmer
Of the fading sunset thus.

My colleagues will be encouraged
To know I've trod on ahead—
Just enough to share my story,
And help someone like me in need.

So hence the day is young indeed—
The page is freshly begun.
What for my Master shall I do?
But wait on the waiting Son?

The One who's done it all for me
So many times before!
He'll need to do it again, you see
Just like He's done before.

*(continued)*

*Brenda A. Kemper Purdy*

## OPENING MY HEART TO GOD

And when the time comes to say, "Well done,"
I'm sure He'll say to me—
"Come up higher, now, My Daughter!
You've done your best for Me!"

And really that's only all that He requires
Is your and my best when things are blue.
For if things were always rosy then,
We'd always know just what to do!

And if I know the Master right,
He's the kind that says,— "Do your best, Children!"
"But in the long run,— it's how you run the race that counts!"
So cheer up weary pilgrim—the time is **now!**

Christ did not forsake his old flock
And He'll not forsake us at **this time!**
For Christ is calling each one of us
**To stand for truth alone!**

Are you willing to be counted among
His disciples—regardless of their renown?
To take your stand with the small band
Marching to Zion today?

*(continued)*

*Brenda A. Kemper Purdy*

The Saints Are Home at Last!

>It won't be long till we all are home,
>And we each will thrill to say—
>With one felt voice ringing out across the sea of glass—
>***"We've made it home to be with Jesus at last!"***
>
>***"To stay forevermore! To stay! Praise God! Praise God!***
>***Our Savior, and Lord, and Guide, and King—***
>***Has vindicated the character of God supreme!***
>***And all the saints are home at last!"***
>
>***Praise the Lord! Praise the Lord! And praise the Lord again!***
>***Thank You, God, the Father! Thank You, Jesus! And thank You, Holy Spirit—the Three In One!***
>
>**The End!**

# **Direction**

I am weak, and Thou art strong.
Help me, Father, to get along.
Sometimes it seems so fully wrong
That guilt just rears its head full strong!

Why, God, do You manifest Yourself so strong,
When others may cry and sigh so long?

"This is not the purpose, Child, of your decision to come along.
But you must look up to where you last saw truth—
And there is where you now belong!"

**The End!**

*Written for devotions about 7:30 AM on February 28, 2012.*

# GUARD THE ENTRANCE

When do we begin? When do we start?
Will people believe it? Will people see it?
From the heart?

We are on the journey ***now,***
Please, let's not depart!—
We are all together now, and doing it right from the start!

Isn't that the part?
For if one second's lost—
Satan will creep in!

We now must guard the entrance,
Of the doorways to besetting sins—for preventing entrance is key—
For all persons' victories!

**The End**

*Written about 7:45 AM on February 28, 2012, for personal devotions; amended slightly on June 15, 2020.*

*Brenda A. Kemper Purdy*

# GLORY BE

***GLORY BE FOR THE SAVIOR*** Who paid the price!
Finally soon—we all shall rest—
In our eternal home called **HAPPINESS**.
And though the way seem oft so steep,
And paths are rocky beneath the feet—
We can only know that Jesus lives,
And wants to give us better lives!

So listen up my friends, today—
If you will harden not your hearts, and pray—
Our Lord and Savior will come to say,
"Open up the door of your hearts and let **Me** stay!"
Praise God above for this chance to glory free—
One always ***CAN CHOOSE THAT GOD'S GLORY BE!***

**The End**

*Written just about midnight on a Friday evening, March 2, 2012; amended slightly on Monday, June 15, 2020, and Thursday, June 18, 2020, and finally finished on Friday, September 4, 2020, a Preparation Day for the Sabbath.*

*Brenda A. Kemper Purdy*

*Brenda A. Kemper Purdy*

# To Reap the Golden Harvest

**"Come down from the mountaintop,"**

I hear my Savior say.
**"You can't stay up there always."**
**"It's just for today."**

*For sometimes I need to realize*
*That life is just so plain*
*And I must trust my Savior*
*In spite of all the rain.*

***So when it starts to get fearful,***
***And things seem to be uptight,***
***What one needs to remember is***
***That God will make all things right!***

*For God is in the business*
*Of doing just what He thinks is best.*
*No need to fear when He is near,*
*'Cause you'll surely pass each test—*

*Of preparation for the latter rain.*

*(continued)*

Brenda A. Kemper Purdy

**And to reap the golden harvest**
In our lives that were so plain—
*We must journey on to Canaan—*
*Where we'll be at peace again!*

**The End!**

*Written May 19, 2012; Modified August 16, 2013;*
*December 4, 2013; and on July 26, 2019.*

# Longing for God

**Longing for You, oh God, to wipe my tears away;**
**Longing for You, oh God, to come on Your great Day.**
**Longing to be, oh God, like You, that I may go**
**Home to reside with You, oh God, I'm longing so!!!**


Longing it seems, for the process to become complete
Of that which You'd started long ago, far off and oh, so sweet.
But now seems distant, uncertain, and out of sync.
And as I look at my life closely, perhaps not clean enough.

I see so many countless times I've failed the mark;
So many times I've not passed the test
And needed to go around Mt. Sinai again,
That as I look and stare over my time,
I've squandered so much in negative slime.

*(continued)*

## OPENING MY HEART TO GOD

I feel helpless and unsure of my future divine.
Will I really ever overcome as I ought?
Or be victorious with every onslaught?
Or do I **make** the trouble happen—

By doubting and fear, and questioning Your promises
Which You've given so clear?
Oh, Lord, help me know my soul, and that right well;
Make me know purity to avoid certain hell.

For have You not told us to work out—
Our salvation with fear and trembling to boot?
Well, Lord, here I am. Please take out every evil root
That may still lodge in my heart!

Shoot out Your arrows of faith, courage, and love which are able to quench
The fiery darts from the enemy all around!
Help me, oh God, use the Sword of Your Word and Gospel of Peace
To proclaim the Good News of what You've done in my life.

And what You **can** do, in any and all others who put their trust in You,
And are longing to be true to You, too!

*(continued)*

*Brenda A. Kemper Purdy*

Yes, *longing* is my heart's desire.
Fulfill it now, oh God, is my earnest plea!

***Longing* to be whole like You;**
**Fully trusting in Your guidance, and in You complete.**
***Longing* for God to do His perfect work in me—then—**
**I'm *longing* to be with Him soon—my *longing* for God will *never* end!!!**

**The End!**

*Written September 27, 2012, upon arising before devotions; after meditating a while and talking to God!*

*Brenda A. Kemper Purdy*

# Mary's Dilemma—Our Own

Long ago in a town not so unlike ours today,
Was a baby born to a young woman who really knew how to pray.
This woman was of the common lot, but oh so special was she.
At first she didn't realize how great, a responsibility was hers to be.

How could she know? She was just a youth and regarded as a virgin you see—
But when the angel appeared to her, miraculous as could be,
And told her the role she would need to play, down through future's history,
She wavered but a moment at her unique calling—for she knew she needed to receive
The blessing of God in her life somehow, to perform this mighty deed!

So she answered the call of God on her life, just as you and I may do today.

*(continued)*

*Brenda A. Kemper Purdy*

## Mary's Dilemma—Our Own

Oh, we may not be raising up the Son of God,—
But no less,— do we take time to pray?
Do we spend thoughtful hours with this Christ Child,
The only One who can make us
Today like God?
Do we take the time to read and study His Word
So we know what we believe and why?

In small ways and big ways, we are filling our time
With choices to obey or reject this Christ Child divine.
So won't you please reconsider at this time of year,
When all the bustle and hubbub is over and clear,

So that there's time once again to raise one's thoughts high
And choose to be part of this Christ Child's birthday?
When we can renew our goals to be true
To the God who so loved ones like me and like you!

And was born on this earth to show us all how
To live without sinning in perfect union even **now!**
Today He is just as relevant as before,
For without Him there would be no promise for sure—

*(continued)*

*Brenda A. Kemper Purdy*

## OPENING MY HEART TO GOD

That He would return to take His children known,
To be with Him forever in our bright, eternal home.

**The End!**

*Written Friday, December 21, 2012, specifically for the St. Helena Seventh-day Adventist Church Christmas Program on Sabbath, December 22, 2012. It took about an hour to compose. Praise God!*

*Brenda A. Kemper Purdy*

# A Belated Birthday Bouquet

*For you~~~~*

*A belated bouquet for your birthday.*

Sweet and lovely flowers
With warm, loving wishes and prayers
That your day was richly blessed
Throughout all your passing hours!

And that the new year will unfold
To bring you countless joy untold.
Obeying the divine master plan given,
And staying in tune with all its instruction
To win the ultimate life-long race!

By becoming cornerstones and gems,— polished—
After the similitude of a palace!
And accepting this belated birthday bouquet
That's a greeting just for you today

*(continued)*

*Brenda A. Kemper Purdy*

*OPENING MY HEART TO GOD*

To know you're very much loved—

And wished many blessings from above!

**The End!**

*Written on December 25 and 26, 2012; dedicated to a girlfriend for her birthday [December 19], and also to **ALL** my sisters in Christ.*

# To a Friend

**When the day is done,**
**And the time is gone,**
**What stays behind is what really matters, friend.**
**For if you seek, you will find.**

And even at the evening's end,
That Truth wins out
When followed friend! Then—
Because the day is upon us,

The thoughts and feelings of the day,
Thoughts that don't easily fade away
Are replaced by thoughts of faith and trust,
Knowing one has entrusted all to Christ.

For victory that will not cease!
Victory, that is worth the cost!
For victory we strive to obtain,
To keep to the prize and then to win!

The joy of realizing this, friend, brings
Much health, happiness, and every such thing.
For Jesus wants us to receive

*(continued)*

*Brenda A. Kemper Purdy*

*OPENING MY HEART TO GOD*

What only He can truly give.

So when all is said and done,
And the time has forever gone,
What really matters then, friend,
Is do you really in the end "belong"?

Belong to Jesus, full and free;
Belong to Jesus, kind and pure you see.
Belong to Jesus, willing to die;
Belong to Jesus Who gave His life for you?!!

**May we each be willing—and for this I trust.**

**Complete surrender for "*belonging*," friend, is always a MUST.**

**You'll reap happiness and joy beyond end—**

**When you surrender all to Christ, my friend!**

**The End!**

*Written January 23, 2013 and finished by 8:30 PM. Dedicated to a friend who was ill, and to **all** my friends as well. Modified on December 4, 2013.*

*Brenda A. Kemper Purdy*

# "Addicted"

What am I **addicted** to?
Is it love that will take me through?
Through to the kingdom shining bright
Where never a dark and lonely night
Can reach and touch a lonely soul like I?
And where down deep inside the heart does cry?

Nearly smothered by the burdens it bears,
Wondering when time and choice will empty the cares
And cast them on the great Burden-bearer
To be carried and released to the great Source of Power
That will take and make me more like Him,
Ready to gain victory, e'en though it may seem slim?

Jesus still offers hope to ones like me,
Bright with promise for all to see.
As long as I keep looking to Him,
He will always keep caring for me, and then
The union that's made will now begin
To become solidly, purposely, addicted to Him!

And in the continuing battle ahead—
**Please, Lord,** help me—

*(continued)*

*Brenda A. Kemper Purdy*

## OPENING MY HEART TO GOD

    as You've always led.
    Take my heart and make it true
    Fully addicted always, Lord—
    to *You!*

**The End!**

*Written January 23, 2013, during 9 PM and 10:30 PM, taking about thirty to forty-five minutes to compose. Modified Feb 14, 2013; December 4, 2013; and June 4, 2015. The idea came to me because of someone who seemed to be addicted to a game.*
*Hence, the spin-off poem.*

# Sealed into Thy Eternal Lasting Covenant

**Seal me, Lord, into Thy eternal lasting covenant—**
Where moth and rust do not corrupt;
Where silver and gold are not an issue,
And joy and attitude are always up!

This seal You place on me, Lord, I find
Sets me apart from others not of like mind.
For where your treasures are, the heart will follow
And moth and rust will then not wallow!

Instead—a new, complete, and glorious home
Where moth and rust can never roam.
What peace and glory then I'll share
Beside Jesus' throne with **Him** right there!

So seal me now, I pray, Dear Lord—
Keep me ever in Thy everlasting Word.

*(continued)*

*Brenda A. Kemper Purdy*

And trusting You for every need,
Let me be *sealed into Thy eternal lasting covenant*—
indeed!

**The End!**

*Written on February 23, 2013, as part of early morning devotions to the Lord. It took about forty minutes to compose. The Holy Spirit gave this to me, as I prayed He would inspire. Thank You, Jesus the Son, Father, and Holy Spirit, the "Three In One"! Praise God!!!*

*Brenda A. Kemper Purdy*

# Dependence on the Lord

This morning, Lord, as I sit at my desk—
I somehow wonder that I'm not at rest.
For as I am writing these words to You,
**I am trusting You to bring me through**

**To victory, Jesus, for this is what I desire:**
*To be like You and aspire*
to the person You want for me to become.
Just for today—please, Lord, lead me home—

To Your heart full of love and compassion, too,
*Where I will see my brothers and sisters, like* **You** *do.*
And lift me up out of myself
Into a glorious body in which **You** dwell.

And then make me do the things **You** would do,
And say just what **You** want for me to say,
Just now, my LORD, just for today—
***Even on this Thy holy Sabbath Day!***

*(continued)*

*Brenda A. Kemper Purdy*

*OPENING MY HEART TO GOD*

As I surrender fully to **You** right now,
Help me to realize, beyond a shadow of doubt,
**That You are truly with me, and that** ***You will carry me,***
*So that You will live in and through me today, is my prayer!*


Thank You, Jesus, for hearing me here,
And for making it come true, as Your will to do.
And praise You, God, for all **You** have done,
*and for all You are about to do through Your Son!*


**And praise You, Holy Spirit, just now, You THREE,**
**Count me in with ALL of You now, OK?**
**Praise God!!!**
**PTL!!! (Praise the Lord!!!)**


**The End!**


*Written Sabbath, March 2, 2013, during devotions and prayer early in the morning before SS and Church; After praying, it took about thirty minutes to compose. I needed to hurry to finish getting ready for church,*

*(continued)*

*but I had asked the Holy Spirit to give me something to write for Him, and He did. I amended this on March 28, 2013, and slightly amended it also during devotions on Friday, August 23, 2019, the Preparation Day for the Sabbath!*

# *Easter Morning Revival—Will It Last?*

Easter morn prepares to dawn.
So bright and clear the sky.
Stars are out. The canopy's shown—
Of millions of lights so brilliant and high!

Something unexpected is in the air,
just what, the disciples don't know—
They are gathered together because of some **fear**
For their very own lives don't you know?

One might think the lives of the early church
Were so privileged to know Christ our Lord.
*But isn't one privileged today to come close*
**To the One, Passionate, Incarnate Word?**

Back then the trial proposed great search
Into the disciples broken hearts—
Were they more ready than we are today?
To take up the Cross and restart?

Start down the long road of true sacrifice—
With dedication to all mankind

*(continued)*

*Brenda A. Kemper Purdy*

Loving God supremely first you know
Then others as they'd journey to find—

**That perfect balance the Master taught**
The disciples so slowly learned each day.
Each day with the Savior so far from them now—
But restart they must do to love and obey!

For Jesus had spoken of this very *day*
That would come to **us all**, somehow.
Time had come,—the third day—
Would Jesus arise—just as He said time would allow?

**But wait!—What is the news? (Jesus has risen! 'Tis true!)**
What **JOY** now abounds and resides in the hearts
Of the men who were the chosen few!
And of those who recalled Jesus' plain, simple words…

*"I Am the Resurrection and the Life. He that believeth in*
*Me, though he were dead, yet shall he live." (John 11:25)*

With the Resurrection past and Jesus as proof
No need now to fear death again!

*(continued)*

*Brenda A. Kemper Purdy*

Easter Morning Revival—Will It Last?

**"Death's been swallowed up in victory!"**
Is now the disciples joy-filled refrain!

**Will it last?**—One might think—
All this joy and fervent actions they were,
That of telling the Good News to the then-known world,
Spreading hope of the **Resurrection** and **Eternal Life** for sure!

*Following the tear-stained banner of Christ*
To reach their eternal home,
Would take everything the disciples could muster
*To follow wherever God led them* <u>**THAT MORN!**</u>

**Did it last for *them*? Will it last for *you*?** —
Records show most of the twelve were faithful and true.
Judas betrayed **HIM**. How about you?
**Will you take a stand for the *Resurrected LORD*?**

**Will you fully surrender, even now—anew?**
**Each day that one must constantly, vigilantly pursue**
**The cross that is waiting for each of us to bear,**
**Will you follow, surrendering, everything to *HIS CARE*?**

*(continued)*

*Brenda A. Kemper Purdy*

*OPENING MY HEART TO GOD*

O friend, as you calculate your time today,
**Please think of Jesus and what He's done for you,**
Given you hope everlasting—
And **Eternal Life** too—!

***And please—in the quiet of your hearts just now,***
***Make Easter Morning Revival come true***
***for you, too!—***
***Won't you—?***

**The End!**

*Started this poem March 13, 2013, about 8:30 PM on my way home from prayer meeting in the car, because the Church secretary had asked me to write a poem for the Easter Program. I did not finish then, but by about 8 PM, March 24, 2013; and read it at the St. Helena Seventh-day Adventist Church Easter Program on Sabbath, March 30, 2013.*

Brenda A. Kemper Purdy

# Brenda's Personal Devotions

Dear Lord, to You I come with nothing to bring—
I cling to all I have—my sins, my guilt, my past.
Lord—I'm not worthy to be called **Your** child—or to
be made holy,
For I am so unclean with past mistakes, selfishness,
pride, jealousy, unbelief, and disobedience!
How could **You** love one such as me??

I cannot see how I fit in the story of the sinner woman
Who brought the alabaster box to **You**
And sacrificed her pride to give it,
Risked her faith in **Your** acceptance,
Or possible rejection of her life, to **You**.
Where could I possibly fit in, **God?**

Where? Please tell. Or show me.
Because I am pharisaical and condemn myself already.
I doubt and question my sincerity.
Help me, Jesus!
I don't want to slide further down into the pit [or abyss]
Where I'll never see the answer "why", to my cry—
Help! Help! Help!

*(continued)*

*Brenda A. Kemper Purdy*

## OPENING MY HEART TO GOD

I come naked to the cross.
There's nothing I can bring.
I ponder **life** without **You**….
What would **life** be without **You**, Lord?
Without Your **guidance** in my **life** thus far?
Where would I be and what would I have become?
Would I really still be alive?
I ponder **life** at all.

What's the meaning of it?
Where am I?
And where am I headed?
Where have I been?
Where am I going?

*O God! My soul cries out to You!*
*Please—I cannot handle my thoughts—they are too much for me.*
*I am not worthy to think, except I am thankful to Thee I am free to think,*
*And choose to think what I want!*

Please help me know **Your thoughts** for my mind
that are higher than my own.
Help me to keep **You** ever in my heart and on my mind
to rule on my heart's throne.

*(continued)*

*Brenda A. Kemper Purdy*

I praise **You** that **You** have not given up on me yet!
And that where I fit into this story is simply representative of a sinner's forgiven regrets—
Not much or a little, but somewhere in-between.
For **Jesus** ate at the home of Simon, and there were others there that were seen.

So I won't be the greatest or least perhaps—but somewhere in-between—
Because I do lean toward the fact that I appreciate what **You** have done for me,
**Lord**, today, more than ever before—
And perhaps to some of the degree this woman experienced too, you see.

I pray it is more than Simon's amount, however.
**Jesus**, though, was willing to forgive even Simon, if he desired this,
For the gospel of the kingdom of heaven is for anyone willing to receive it.
So it boils down to today—

*What am I going to do with You in my life today, Lord?*
Am I thankful **You are my all in all today?**
Have I surrendered my weakness of pride and doubt and disbelief—

*(continued)*

## OPENING MY HEART TO GOD

Or unbelief in **Your promises** to carry me through to
**victory in You today?**

*Please, Lord,* *I do this, right now—surrender all.*
*I confess these sins to* ***You****.*
**Thank You,** Jesus—help me **now.**
Try me to see if there be any wicked way in me too.

Yes, I am unworthy. But praise **God**,
All of us really do fit into this story's category
somewhere!
(Hopefully, for the better results)
So, **Lord**, I pray today,

Help me to say and stay close by **You**
**And keep You inside me, I pray.**
Help me obey **You** and follow every pathway
where **You** lead me today.

Thank **You, Father**, for giving me **Jesus**
to walk with and **Partner** with on my journey today.
Keep me focused on duty and **His** will to obey.
Give me the **Holy Spirit** to abide with me too,

And never let go of my hand in ***Yours,***
So that today will be *victorious and happy,*

*(continued)*

> *peaceful and calm,*
> *efficient and energetic,*
> **With Jesus at my helm!**

> **Praise God!**
> **Praise Jesus!**
> **Praise Holy Spirit!**
> ***Three In One! The great THREE! The eternal God!***
> ***Amen!***

> **The End!**

*Written March 28, 2013 about 5 AM after reading the passage of a sinful woman forgiven, in Luke 7:36–50, during personal devotions.*

*Brenda A. Kemper Purdy*

# INNER REFLECTIONS

Sometimes I wonder of late—, many times now,
How people can do the things that they do?
But somehow Jesus is teaching me thus—
To mind my own business and keep to His trust—

Certain things people do that *irritate* me so
Which I really don't understand why—
That if they really loved Jesus
They would treat me in such a way!

But God is telling me to *let these things go*
To the graveyard of His infinite, almighty *love* and *know*
Where Jesus will judge everything great and small
*On that Day—the great Judgment Day of all!*

He wants me to work, and He wants me to pray;
Work because night will soon be turned into day.
And pray because I need to deeper care
In a more specific and **Christlike way!**

To give others the benefit of the doubt for starters
*And leave the judgment calls totally to His control*

*(continued)*

To experience the true meaning of love in a way
That I've never experienced as such before this day.

To learn that communication is important, and honesty the key.
No masquerade shows for you or for me!
And clarity must always be clothed in love,
So there's always a peace that satisfies from above.

When efforts are put forth to this end,
**Of communicating the truth of a matter to a trustworthy *Friend*,**
I may experience the true joy **Jesus** talks about in **His Word—**
And know of a surety that I ***am*** on the narrow road!

**The End!**

---

*Written during the middle of the night when I arose to pray and meditate on May 6, 2013. I began approximately 1:10 AM and finished about 2:20 AM, but I typed and modified some more, and was done about 5:40 AM, amending slightly on Friday, August 23, 2019 (The Preparation Day for the Sabbath). PRAISE GOD!*

*Brenda A. Kemper Purdy*

# *To God Be the Glory*

To God be the glory!
My life I desire to make
With all my thoughts, actions, and emotions
Within me which truly relate.

To the way I live and
The way I do.
All for Jesus
Is such a righteous move!

But can I really think—what You want me to think, O Lord?
And **You** do the character part?
Of making me relate to others
With **joy** within my heart?

And to all my earthly problems
As workmen for my fate
So that Christ's perfect life may dwell within me—
And work inside me to remake.

To give me a perfect heart!
I do not see ***how*** this ***must*** be—?

*(continued)*

*Brenda A. Kemper Purdy*

To God Be the Glory

> God seeing the end from the beginning.
> He wants to offer us eternal life!
> And from the beginning throughout eternity
> God wins for us the **VICTORY!**

> But this much I truly know:
> Jesus walks beside me now
> Guiding my steps somehow,
> As long as I am *willing*

> **To give to *Him my all!***
> *Jesus* makes my efforts be just right,
> And helps me when I fall—
> To overcome each tiny thing
> That *irritates* us *ALL!*—

> So I am not the *only* one
> To whom God gives this call—
> ***You, too, can be placed upright***
> ***To never, never,—fall!***

> And to all my earthly problems
> As workmen of my fate—
> I would say just now that ***Christ abides*—,**
> **And is inside of me—**

*(continued)*

*Brenda A. Kemper Purdy*

*OPENING MY HEART TO GOD*

**To perfect my willing heart!**

So you, too, can have a perfect heart,
And then ***abide in Christ*—**
And join with me to walk that narrow road,
Where each of us must start—

Resting confidently in **Him—**
**While trusting Christ to remake,—**
**Our sinful, contrite, heart!**

**The End!**

*Written August 16, 2013, and sung with a friend to a certain melody, on Sabbath, August 17, 2013, in the St. Helena Seventh-day Adventist Church.*

*Brenda A. Kemper Purdy*

# To the Unsighted...

**A creed that's very special**
To rouse the blind man's muscle
Is the one to look into the face
Of one that's given so much grace.
Grace to carry the blind man home;
Grace for the sightless to now freely roam—

**In fullness and completeness— to destiny's door!**

Grace will help one now to easily soar—
And raise the banner of love so divine—
That gives victory and more,
**Giving sight to the blind!**

**The End!**

*This poem was created with the "Phone Faith" participants in mind sometime during 2013–2014, when I recorded out loud, portions of scripture for my blind friends.*

*Brenda A. Kemper Purdy*

# Dedicated to My Blind Friends

O to see the depths of life
When one can work without the strife
Of fear and worry clinging so
That one cannot further, deeper go—

Into the work that God had planned
For each one's life within the span
Of love and service for mankind,
Without the din and roar to find—.

From sand that lines the oceans wide
And brings small gifts direct from tide,
That sees the land from shore to shore
And the bounty God has in store,

Makes me the greater, deeper know
God's love within **my** life somehow.
And makes me yearn for deeper sight
That goes beyond this world so trite—

In to the world of darkness and depths unknown;
Of courage, confidence, and love that's shown.

*(continued)*

Brenda A. Kemper Purdy

Dedicated to My Blind Friends

So one can see from heaven above
**The wisdom God ordained to give with love.**

And be recipient of God's love and grace,
To finally, fully, deeper face
The One who truly persevered the race
**Between light and darkness *He* had to face**

To offer the love of **redeeming grace!**
With friends that make me sure,
***Such a heaven is for those who endure.***
And then we'll see the **beauty** of each one's life,

**How God has walked beside them in spite of the night!**
And if one doubts of God's wisdom and grace,
We'll know for certain that God has woven each of us—
Into **His glorious masterpiece!!!**

**The End!**

*God granted this poem to me on September 22, 2013, during morning watch. It took 1 ½ hours to compose, and it was amended slightly Sunday, September 8, 2019.*

*Brenda A. Kemper Purdy*

# Eyes That Can See

*Also written during time with Jesus on September 22, 2013, in honor of my blind friends, and amended slightly on September 8, 2019.*

Thank You, Lord, for everything!
**We know that You are King**
Who works things out accordingly.
By Your very own Son that brings

**Joy and peace to each one who sings**
**And rejoices with fervor that we are included**
**In the land of endless light—**
**Where we are not deluded!**

A place that will shine with brightness and joy;
A place history plays some parts to destroy
The possible entrance into His righteousness,
With light exceeding every purpose,

To the end of happiness and peace for us.
**Light** made perfect through the faithfulness
Of one who truly realizes
**God's light in lives of all men before us.**

*(continued)*

*Brenda A. Kemper Purdy*

Whether following the walk with Christ alone,
Or just finding out all the past to atone.
**Jesus shines light deep into each one's heart**
**That will explode even the darkest part—**

**Into light that's shining so everyone can be**
*The glow of one whose eyes are set free!*
*And truly become eyes that can see!!!*
**PTL!!! Thank You, Jesus, for this fact—**

That fills the Bible with many acts,
*When Jesus opens the eyes of the blind*
*To heal their eyes so they can find*
*Salvation in Christ for eternal gain!*

**Praise God! and praise God again!**
*Your eyes that can see*
**Now have *complete* vision—**
***When residing with Him eternally!!!***

**The End!**

# What Are You Thankful For?

**What are you thankful for?** Someone asked.
Is it the beauty of the field and grass,
Or perhaps the summer mountain pass,
Which wends its way through tall green pines,
Around cliffs, and up great climbs?

Close to the highway is that sparkling blue-green lake
So gently lapping against the shore.
Majestic snow-covered boulders with the billowy clouds
Against a deep turquoise sky, frame the setting above.
A hike to the pinnacle of the rocks reveals
**Awesome wonder of God the Son!**

**What are you thankful for?** Someone asked.
Is it vigor to run, laugh, and play,
Or perhaps the smile in someone's once-lonely eyes
That you know you've helped to cheer that day?

**What are you thankful for?** Someone asked.
Tasty food, a father's love, and mother's prayers?
That have followed you through the fast-slipping years?
Or perhaps the tender understanding of a patient,

*(continued)*

*Brenda A. Kemper Purdy*

What Are You Thankful For?

>teacher friend,
Who helped and told you what you needed to know right then?

**What are you thankful for?** Someone asked.
Is it Christ who died to set you free?
*Free*, not chained, not burdened by lots of rules,
But *free*. Free to be the individual God wants you to be.
Or perhaps it's His tender love—
That watches over you and cares for you.
*He's always there when you need Him most!*
Just reach up and take His hand.
**Be thankful for Christ!**

**The End!**

*I wrote this perhaps sometime before I was married (in 1976), or later in 2000, when I started writing much more. I amended it slightly on Thursday, November 13, 2014.*

*Brenda A. Kemper Purdy*

# Under the Shadow of the Cross

Under the shadow of the Cross is where I want to be.
Where I am safe from censure, criticism, and harm.
A place to go for peace or retreat;
A place to rest at Jesus feet.
I linger there,— clinging— to His tree,— surrounding
His feet with my tears.
Yes,—surrounding those feet that will set me free with
caresses so tender and dear.
He **will** set me free!

It was because of ***my*** loss,
That Jesus bore the Cross—my own—
And suffered to banish my fears and anxiety.
I see the **shadow** now,—all alone—!
It casts a dark hue o'er me;
But my Savior is waiting to conquer *for* me;
He **will** set me free!

My salvation and victory—o'er sin I'm set free—
**While abiding under the shadow of the Cross.**
There to rest while He patiently removes the ugly dross,
Being purged from my character so faulty and weak.
Praise God—there's a **Cross** of which I can speak—

*(continued)*

*Brenda A. Kemper Purdy*

Of the **victories in Christ** when to **Him I retreat.**
He **is making** me free!

**I stay under the shadow of the Cross.**
For without that **shadow**, there would be no **Cross!**
And without the ***Cross,*** there would be no **hope** for sure
That leads me to choose **everlasting life** so pure.
**Praise God that I'm still under,— the shadow of the Cross!**
Where He will continue to be my constant source of perfect peace!
<u>**He IS *keeping* me free—*while I abide***</u>
<u>***Under the shadow of the Cross!***</u>

**The End!**

*I began this poem on Sabbath morning, September 13, 2008, at 3:25 AM; amended September 21, 2008, at 10:25 PM; September 29, 2008; October 13, 2008, at 8:20 AM; April 15, 2009, at 4:30 PM; and completely finished on February 18, 2014.*

*Brenda A. Kemper Purdy*

# The Gift

Long time ago the Christ Child was born,
So small and precious was He.
The manger stable in Bethlehem
Was His first welcome to earth, you see.

That Babe then grew to manhood,
And became the sinner's **Best Friend.**
He walked and talked and preached each day
Of days ahead that would come to an end.

He told that hard times would soon be upon them,
And He knew they would need a Friend,
To counsel, protect, support, and sustain them
Through tough days ahead that would end.

And at this time of year one remembers
Of days gone by, just when—
A virgin was chosen by God Himself
To mother a child's Best Friend!

We know Christ managed to grow in grace
With each, new, passing day.

*(continued)*

*Brenda A. Kemper Purdy*

## *OPENING MY HEART TO GOD*

What the Christ Child offered then to all—
He's still offering to us today!

He offers freedom from guilt if we only believe
And trust to follow His will.
Christ offers peace amidst the storms of life
That helps **resolve** our problems **still.**

So when **life** goes wrong and **all is lost**
Jesus is the One who redeems the cost—
Of death for sin—the sinner's fair pay,
Christ transacts the **"Gift"** for all who choose today!—

**Please choose wisely, friend.**
One never knows what's ahead.
It behooves each one of us to seek
This **"Gift"** so abundantly shed—

To all who choose Christ today.
**Will you accept the "Gift" He offers to you?**
Or will you *return it*,— unopened,— like new?
**Please choose wisely, friend.**

**So please,**—let the **"Gift"** begin to soften the edges
Of one's heart so set like stone,
And let the **"Gift"** continue to be—

*(continued)*

The Gift

    The overriding part of our **victory**!

To open the **"Gift"** one may choose—
To receive a new heart right away;
One can accept the **"Gift"** so freely given
Or keep the **"Gift"** fully at bay.

Please do not return it unopened, friend.
Instead,—please make the **"Gift"** lodge in your mind today.
Open it and place it on the throne of your heart
To replace the old and make a new start—

With lifegiving energy to all who receive
this precious, solitary, **"Gift"** to conceive
Of new beginnings with Jesus each day—
Please, don't send the **"Gift"** away!

You'll miss the goodness of the Lord if you do!—
So accept and share it with all your friends and neighbors, too.
Then you'll have a peace and contentment without any end—
If you only believe in a Christ that transcends!

And the **"Gift"** will become your very **Best Friend!**

*(continued)*

*Brenda A. Kemper Purdy*

## OPENING MY HEART TO GOD

So,— let the **"Gift"** begin
To soften the edges and purify the soul.
Thus giving the **"Gift"** perfect control.

To change one's thoughts and actions so well
That He, the **"Gift"** will keep one from hell!
Are you thankful, too?
For the **"Gift"** to you?

It's offered so freely
That all you need do,
Is say "Yes" to Christ Jesus
And "No" to the old selfish fool!

**The End!**

*Written on Thursday, December 18, 2014, at approximately 5:45 PM [PDT]; It took about sixty minutes to compose for the St. Helena Seventh-day Adventist Church Christmas Program that year. Amended Monday, July 22, 2019, at 1:45 PM; Monday, July 29, 2019, at 10:10 PM; Tuesday, July 30, 2019, at 5 AM to 10 AM; finally finishing Tuesday, June 16, 2020, at 2:50 AM.*

# Change Me, O God! [1]

*My prayer today, was written on Monday, June 14, 2015, about 3:45 PM, which took approximately thirty minutes to write, when I was realizing all my faults, needing encouragement from fear about not making the "mark," and crying out to God to change my sinful heart—!*

Change me! Please change me, O God!
I cry to You, my only hope!
Please change me and help me—help me to cope
With my sinful un-Christlike self—

That seems so strong in me and so bold,
How can I make it to heaven,
When I must pass through more adversity, I'm told?
The time of Jacob's trouble, that is—

When I must stand alone with You!
I'm fearful I won't make it, see,
'Cause I'm miserable, blind, and naked to Thee.
My character flaws are so pronounced,

I'm really not sure they'll ever get pounced
*(continued)*

*Brenda A. Kemper Purdy*

## OPENING MY HEART TO GOD

To the death of self and sinning in me!
That I'll make the mark of the high calling so free
And abide so that I will never fear

Or question that you're in control or near.
Please change me, O God,—
This wretched soul of mine;
Take my life and keep it Thine!

O help me grasp by faith the truths
That will make me, keep me, pure to lose
Myself in Thee.—As I can see
The only way is for You to be

In my heart with all my being,
Enveloped in Your love, and then foreseeing
The victory You have for me this day—
I must not give up hope along this way!

For what counts most is for me to win
The battle of my cherished sins.
And come to the place of vanquished fear—
Precious Savior—be Thou ever near!

**The End!**

# Change Me, O God! [2]

Change me, O God.
I cannot do it!
Make me pure and clean.
You're listening to me.
I believe it.
So make me understand and see
All the wretchedness I really am to Thee.
Selfish to the core of my heart
Pride of opinion, and more….

Have I changed any?
Perhaps.

It seems so slow, my progress o'er the years!
Perhaps I've grown in You through tears.
And yet there's cherished idols, I fear,
That have been repeatedly yielded, but still….
And I don't understand these issues I face.
I lack use of my faith to obey You,
When You so clearly state—
The need to do differently
In these areas of my fate!

*(continued)*

*Brenda A. Kemper Purdy*

## OPENING MY HEART TO GOD

For though You've promised victory—how can I relate?
When I don't understand the "reasons" for my
obedience of late?
Which You so clearly will direct—
Through Your Word and then through Sister White!

You've said to study not to be ashamed,
And to rightly divide the word of truth.
So surely You will help me now to pursue
The plain path you've set before me.
For though I do not fully know the reasons "why,"
Help my faith to follow Thee,
Where'er You lead me and whatever You ask of me
sublime,
To make my life go through the seasons of time.

### *Epilogue*

Just ahead are rougher waters now—
That will test my purity of soul!
Please, Lord—
Take full control!

And change me, O God!
I cannot do it!
Make me know the joy

*(continued)*

*Brenda A. Kemper Purdy*

And peace You alone can bring
To my soul that now is not willing to cling
To anything that will prevent my life—
From reaching the heaven-sent mark
Of purity, no deceit, no wrinkle, or spot
Found in a life given completely—to God!

The End!

*This was written when I realized my sinful self and my need for doing differently on Tuesday, June 30th, 2015. It was begun at 3:30 AM, while finishing by 5:00 AM. Amended Wednesday, July 22nd, 2015; and also Tuesday, August 27th, 2019.*

*Brenda A. Kemper Purdy*

# Change Me, O God! [3]

**Change me anew,— O God!**
This I pray.
Make me completely like You
Today!
Thank You for listening to my struggling heart,
Learning to trust You not only in part
But whole and completely
From the bottom of my heart!—
Take me and fashion me after Your will,
Make me hear Your voice so quiet and still.
Teach me the way in which I should go.
Strengthen and change me—make me do
The plain path ahead to accomplish your will.
This I long for—to obey Your voice still!
Each time I hear it—help me rejoice with *free will.*
Make me to know the *joy* of Your salvation,
Complete with courage and assurance to deal with
every situation!

**Change me anew—**
Because I've often failed You,
Gotten discouraged and traveled the wrong road
Not only in actions, but in my thoughts.

*(continued)*

*Brenda A. Kemper Purdy*

Negativity, dwelling on problems,
Instead of what God has taught!
Change me anew—
Today to be like You.
I need **You** to do it!
Praise God!
You're willing!
For the indwelling of Your sweet Spirit today—
***Change me anew!***
***This— I pray!***

**The End!**

*My prayer written on July 22, 2015, after the General Conference of Seventh-day Adventists had convened and dismissed. On the way home we were traveling through Nevada. I began about 8 AM, and finished within two hours.*

*Brenda A. Kemper Purdy*

# Wide Open Spaces

There's just something special about wide open spaces.
A peace and beauty simply supplied;
Mountains surrounding the valleys so clear,
And ease of the eyes with greenery dear.
Long distances to see with no obstruction in view;
Fresh air; no smog; just the road and you!
Reminding me of this journey of life
We complicate with too much strife!
But far as the eye can see
One feels the yearning to be free!

**The End!**

*This was written July 22, 2015, while traveling in the car through Nevada. I began at 11 AM and finished 11:15 AM.*

# THE ROAD

Traveling down the road a piece
One finds guidelines on the pavement—
Painted white as fleece.
Center lines one after the other with spaces in between
But close enough together to be seen.
This really helps the driver know
Where the curves and straightaways are,
And guides the car by orange and white
To keep in the straightaway on the right!
So much like the Bible are these white lines
Guiding me through the pathway of time!

*Written on July 22, 2015, and done in about fifteen minutes while traveling in Nevada; started about 11:20 AM and finished about 11:35 AM.*

*Brenda A. Kemper Purdy*

# Remember

**Help us remember how you lead us, Lord!**
Take our lives and make them Yours.
We are fallible and finite it seems,
Make us to value what *You* dream.

For us to become in every way like *You*,
Teach us to trust *You* and follow through
With actions that characterize the prize
Of the high calling of Christ in our lives!

To reach the goal of this great race,
**Remember to help us in our weak state!**
Help us do the things so true
That we've learned before but somehow blew!

*Don't ever give up on us, Lord! Please!*
*We long to be perfect and all for Thee!*
**Help us remember Your Word ever sure,**
*To make our lives completely pure.*

And to make us live like *You* want us to.
Please, Lord, now, we surrender anew.
**Remember our choices to become like *You*.**

*(continued)*

Brenda A. Kemper Purdy

# Remember

**Help us remember *we cannot live without You*—**

Working in our lives to make them true—
True to **Your Word** which comforts us now.
True to follow, on the road somehow—
**Remembering Your teaching in each of our lives.**

**And help us remember to deal gently with ourselves—**
As we strive to become one in spirit, mind, and soul,
While we let *You* take full and complete control!
Bless us, Lord! **Remember our fate.**

Teach us to trust *You* and how to relate
To each other with unselfish, giving, and love—
So we may soon enter into the realms above.
Thank You, Lord, for all You've done

To make us clean and truly one
With **Your** spirit, body, and mind.
**Thank You for remembering to make us kind!**
**And when we doubt, help us remember the way to find out!**

Thank You, Jesus, for doing this for us,
Something we cannot do without **trust**.

*(continued)*

*Brenda A. Kemper Purdy*

*OPENING MY HEART TO GOD*

**Please help us remember when times get tough**
To choose *You* over all the *stuff*

That so easily besets our efforts here.
**Help us remember to make *You* dear.**
Dearer than any besetting sin,
Help us remember to let *You* in!

Then we can walk more closely with *You*,
And gain the victory so much overdue!
**So remember us gently, Lord, I pray.**
**Thank You for teaching us all this today!**

**The End!**

*I wrote this poem on Monday evening, July 27, 2015, while Les was taking a walk. I kept writing and concluded about 12:20 AM on July 28, 2015. This is my attitude about that day's experience with Jesus! PTL!!! Amended slightly on Friday, July 31, 2015; November 24, 2015; and on Thursday, August 29, 2019.*

*Brenda A. Kemper Purdy*

# JUDGMENT

Sometimes it seems death is final.
But truth is, the life we lived before—
Will determine whether death reigns eternal,
And God only is the judge of yore.

Yore when one would have the chance
To choose the path to travel.
How important then **time** must be
To make the choice eternal!

**We must not sit in God's judgment seat!**
When time has stopped, and then—
God will allow us to judge men's records,—and over angels' feet,
And how they chose to sin!

When it's all said and done,
God only is the One—
Who knows the heart that's shrouded
In choices that are somewhat clouded.

**And we are not to judge anyone's motive**
To determine one's fate under the sun.

*(continued)*

*Brenda A. Kemper Purdy*

*But we are to judge only types of behavior*
*As wise or foolish Christian endeavor.*

So we do agree God's love is **unconditional,**
**In that He loves us whether we sin or not.**
*But our love for Him—it is relational.*
*And we must choose to obey Him, if we love at all.*

*So being a Christian is not only based on His love for us,*
*It is based on our love for Christ.*
**And if we love Him, we will keep His commands**
**That we may daily have eternal life—**

**And live in that eternal land!**

**The End!**

*Written July 31, 2015, the year of the General Conference of Seventh-day Adventists which we were blessed to be able to attend.*

# Riley, the Cat

There once was a loving cat named Riley.
He brought so many deep smiles!
His sweet little spirit was truly blessed,
And we are grateful he will soon be at rest.

At rest from the ravages of illness,
The loss of appetite with suffering so sadly.
The loss of energy and contentedness,
That meant so much to Riley mostly!

So today we gather in the memory
Of a pet, companion, and friend.
We longingly wait for the redemption
When at Christ's coming we'll meet,

Not only our Savior and King—
But I believe we will meet Riley again!
When we ask Jesus to re-create
Our own beloved Riley, and friend!

The beautiful, golden yellow stripes
Are like bright rays of sunshine,
Giving love at every stroke of fur.

*(continued)*

*Brenda A. Kemper Purdy*

*OPENING MY HEART TO GOD*

The purring only magnifies his happiness

In living with his people friends!
Erik showered him with love and goodness—
Manifested in his length of life on this earth.
We will miss Riley's quiet, steadfast adoration
To those who gave him so much attention!
But this we know that Riley somehow
Will rest in peace-like sleep,
Even as Jesus said Lazarus was "sleeping."

So we trust Riley to our dear Savior's keeping
To present to Erik and others someday
A re-created pet in perfect glory, that will say,
"Thank you, Erik!" "Thank you, friends!"

"We now each will enjoy eternal bliss!"
So, thank **You**, Lord, for giving Riley to us,
A faithful, loving companion!
"Sleep, sweet friend,—till the Morning of the Great
Resurrection!!"

**The End!**

*Erik, a good friend of ours, requested I write a poem in honor of his beloved cat, Riley. So the Lord gave this*

*(continued)*

*Brenda A. Kemper Purdy*

Riley, the Cat

> *poem to me on September 14, 2015. It was amended slightly on November 22, 2015, and Thursday, October 22, 2020. We took Riley to the vet and he went to sleep on November 25, 2015.*

# Our Friend, Arno

*There is a young man named Arno*
*Who is amiable like one might be.*
*We met him one day at a mutual friend's home*
*And invited him to **our** home, you see.*

*He soon became our devoted friend*
*And would join us regularly*
*To attend functions, church, or wherever we'd go*
*Enjoying food with us occasionally, too.*

*Over time, he has been considerate*
*In His courtesies to us, we know—*
*That we really miss him generally*
*When unable to accompany us so.*

*Thank you, Arno, for being our friend.*
*You've been such a blessing to know*
*That you've become like an adopted son to us*
*To help fill our childless lives here below.*

*(continued)*

Brenda A. Kemper Purdy

Our Friend, Arno

*May the good Lord give you the desires
Of your heart when delighting in God's love
So that you, Arno, will taste of God's goodness
And experience true friendship—a gift from above!*

*Today—may we each come to realize
There is such a neat guy here with us.
Ang that being his friend is an honor and privilege
For all he meets and greets with us!*

*Just now we pray a special blessing rest upon Arno,
That all of us will meet around God's throne
To reign with Jesus forever and ever
As brothers and sisters in the Lord—*

*Down the corridors of time
Throughout eternity sublime;*

*(continued)*

*Brenda A. Kemper Purdy*

*And truly experience the joy of loving one another,*
*And Jesus Christ, our "Elder Brother"!*

**The End!**

*Started writing Wednesday, February 12, 2020, and finished Friday before Sabbath, February 14, 2020; It was amended Saturday night, February 15, 2020; Sunday, February 16, 2020; Thursday, October 22, 2020; finally finishing Thursday, January 14, 2021.*

# Am I Ready for Heaven?

**Am I ready for heaven?**
Where perfect love reigns?
Do I reflect His love to others
With peace and harmony?
Supporting all the positive ways
That shine out through you and me?

**Am I ready for heaven?**
To live forevermore,
With joy and peaceful abiding,
In the One who loves me so?

**Am I ready to walk that sea of glass**
**And behold the Savior's face?**
Do I really, fully, completely trust
In the One that's won the race?

**Am I ready to die and not give in**
For truth that keeps me free?

*(continued)*

*Brenda A. Kemper Purdy*

Do I practice what I preach each day?
To make the rafter's ring?

**Am I ready for heaven?**
I still must ask myself.
Am I striving to be forgiven
Of every blot of little sin?
And does time take on new meaning
When the day has just begun?

**Am I ready for heaven?**
Is this my sincere desire?
To live each moment fully clothed
In God's blood-washed robe made white through cleansing fires?
Is my character pure and clean today?
Free from stain, spot, or evil desires?

**Am I ready for heaven? I cry—**
Now that I've been washed in His blood and tested?
Do I come out pure gold with absolutely no dross?
And leave my old life behind of restlessness?

**By God's grace, I <u>am</u> ready for heaven!**
Ready to hear the words,

*(continued)*

Am I Ready for Heaven?

**"Well done, My good and faithful servant—
Enter now into the joy of your Lord!"**

**The End!**

*I wrote this on Sabbath, October 10, 2015, about 4–5 AM; amended on Sunday, October 11, 2015, at 5:30 PM; and on Tuesday, August 20, 2019, at 9:51 PM.*

*Brenda A. Kemper Purdy*

# *Sequel*
## to "*Am I Ready for Heaven?*"

*This can happen only through faith in Christ,*
*And total surrender each moment—*
*"The just shall live by faith," the Bible says,*
*Faith in the Son of God who's done it!*

*Who's lived the life for me to have.*
*And Who will take me up for certain.*
*When all is said and done by faith today,*
*I **am** ready to go to heaven!*

**Praise God for what He's done!**

***The End!***

*Written sometime after the creation of "Am I Ready for Heaven?"*

Brenda A. Kemper Purdy

# Rebirth

At this time of year, let all come to know
The One Reason for the Season—
The Christ Child below
Who came to this earth!

To show us the *rebirth*—
**We each must follow.**
Yet somehow we resist
This process amiss.

We must look into our hearts of sorrow to permit
The Christ Child to take over our hearts—
Just every little bit!
Does He have mine today? Does He have yours?

I must ask myself ***Who knows***
The heart better than anyone?
When it comes to control—
Control of our choices?

So often overlooked?
Do we have the right?
To search deep inside?

*(continued)*

*Brenda A. Kemper Purdy*

# OPENING MY HEART TO GOD

To surrender so deeply?

That all of our pride
Is crushed by the beauty
Of One's Life so well-lived?
That all of our hearts

We are willing to give?—
**Rebirth it must be—**
*For you and for me.*
Examine one's life! Is it totally fine?

To trust without worry?
To rest, not repine?
Do I cast all my cares?
On the Christ Child divine?

Is my hope in the Christ Child
Really, really mine?
Am I totally surrendered?
To **His life** so sublime?

Let's pause for a moment——
What do I see?
When I look deep inside
Where corrupt thinking may be?

*(continued)*

# Rebirth

Am I totally focused?
To yield all my pride?
Pride of my opinion
Selfish and loud?—

Pride of ability
To conquer on my own?
Am I thinking pure thoughts
That are without blame?

Do I judge one another
To keep ahead of the game?
Or do I blame the same person—
Again and again?

Am I sorry for hurting
Your children as well?
A friend or my spouse or my child—
**Do I cast into hell?**

What about influence?
Do I gossip as one?
Who neither knows the truth—
And exaggerates all?

Am I carrying my feelings

*(continued)*

## OPENING MY HEART TO GOD

On my shoulder somehow?
Am I sensitive to others' feelings?
Do I care enough without?

Do I trust to myself?
Or do I let Jesus take over?——
**Rebirth** is what I really want **this Christmas**—
A time of full surrender!

What more can I ask for?
When I pause to remember—
Just what the Christ Child has done for me?
He longs for me to be truly free.

Conquering doubt and distrust!
We really, really must genuinely see—
That **rebirth** is what's needed—
*For you, and for me.*

So as I worship this Christmas season
May all I do and am and know,
Be worth the priceless *GIFT* He **gave** to us—
**A LIFE** born so long ago!

Into this darkened pit of sin,
**A LIFE** for us was in heart reborn each day!

*(continued)*

*Brenda A. Kemper Purdy*

# Rebirth

Just as we have the privilege now of doing.
Let us not spurn **Him** away!

And let us not reject this ***rebirth;***
We must experience it ***daily.***
The Christ Child in us,
That we may love just as freely!

Take a moment right now
To make this choice
We each must make—
To be able to rejoice!

**Rejoice in the victory**
Granted each one!
Rejoice in the peace
Found only through the Baby Son!

Now living in heaven,
Waiting for you and me
To reflect all the Divine merits
Of *rebirth*, you see!

So peace will reign,
And no longer we'll be
Tossed to and fro

*(continued)*

## OPENING MY HEART TO GOD

By our uncertainty.

For in this world we each do live
In a shadow of things to come—.
Won't it be glorious
When at last we're all ***home?***

Seek now to trust Him;
**NOW** is the time!
***Rebirth*** is certain
When we surrender to **Him**!

*Casting our helpless soul upon Jesus,*
*Clinging to His grace,*
*Till one day so very soon—*
*We'll see that matchless* **face!**

**The End!**

*Written early Friday morning, December 11, 2015, from about 4:30 AM to 7:45 AM for the St. Helena Seventh-day Adventist Church Christmas Program to be held on Sabbath, December 19, 2015, which is my birthday and 39th wedding anniversary (at the time of this writing)!*

# *Poem in Honor of "Miss Madison"—Our Precious Cat!*

**Little "Miss Madison," we love you.**
You have taught us about God's love.
You purr and purr so truly
Giving love at every stroke!

You purr even when you are sick.
You purr in gratitude for food.
Even when we "stick" you,
You actually purr for us, good!

**We love you, "Miss Madison!"**
We say goodbye to you with trust,
Leaving you in God's hands
To sleep until that **Day**—a must!

On Resurrection Morning
When graves will burst open with life,
I plan to ask Jesus to raise you up too,
So that **all** of God's people and creatures will be made anew!

To live forever without strife,

*(continued)*

*Brenda A. Kemper Purdy*

## OPENING MY HEART TO GOD

This is truly the goal!!—
**Little "Miss Madison," you've managed to show us**
**The great *love* God has for every soul!**

We will always remember what you have taught us,
**Of God's *unconditional love* in our plight.**
How He looks down upon us
With longings and yearnings to support us outright!

Showering *love's* fragrance and warmth to us in the night.
**God is like that! He gives!**
He gives and gives like the purring He creates
Within sweet Madison's heart, throat, and life.

**We *love* you, precious, Little One—**
**"Miss Madison,"— so sweet, kind, and true.**
**You've been like a daughter to us,**
**Even when you did not know!**

**We love you, little "Miss Madison!"**
You've been just like a daughter to us—it's true!
We've held you, fed you, and cuddled you
Like a child of our very own if we had!

And the many long nights you've explored the house—

*(continued)*

Poem in Honor of "Miss Madison"—Our Precious Cat!

Bedrooms, closets, hallway, living room, and kitchen—
You found solace after the new carpet installation,
Which had caused you displacement during the process—

Or storm of ripping out the old carpet—
Moving furniture around, and being displaced in the disarray for a while.
You weathered the changes magnificently,
And learned to appreciate the comfort sweetly!

**How can we let you go?**
For the unconditional love you've given,
We simply have showered back on you—
Teaching us patience, kindness, and forgiveness too.

Thank you, sweet Madison!
That through it all,
When at times you stretched our patience to the limit
By your naughty habits persistent,

**We continued with our loving care for you!**
**Just like <u>*God cares for us too.*</u>**
Never giving up on our evil ways,
To make us like Jesus for all of our days.

*(continued)*

*Brenda A. Kemper Purdy*

## OPENING MY HEART TO GOD

**Thank you, "Miss Madison!"**
You've shown us **and** given us we must say,
The sense of *joy* in **experiencing GOD'S LOVE,**
So abundantly manifest in your sweet life today!

You have learned to give up your nasty habits
Because we have showered you with **LOVE**!
You have become the beautiful kitty we adore,
Showing us miraculous things to behold.

Rest now till Jesus comes—
And calls all of us to join Him in heaven.
Then we'll understand **GOD'S LOVE** more fully
And how you came to richly bless our little home or haven.

**Thank you, "Miss Madison," for your God-given life and *love*!**
Praise God from Whom all blessings flow from above!
Thank You, Lord, for outpouring Your love
**Through little "Miss Madison," a creature we loved here below!**

**The End!**

*(continued)*

# Poem in Honor of "Miss Madison"—Our Precious Cat!

*This was written January 5, 2016, in honor of our kitty, "Miss Madison." I began about 3 AM, finishing about 4:15 AM. It was amended August 12, 2016, from 2 AM—6:15 AM; and also on December 8, 2016. She lived longer than expected, and in August of 2017, we allowed her to go to sleep.*

*"Miss Madison" became our kitty January or February of 2012. She was already twelve years old when we brought her home from the Napa Animal Shelter, and she had been in the shelter 4 months.*

*She was very difficult to train. However, we were persistent in our patience and love for her, and she finally became a very loving cat,—not unlike how God works on people's lives to become loving Christians with all the fruits of the Spirit, and treating our brothers and sisters with love and patience too.*

## *In Christ Alone*

In Christ alone, I am told to fight!
If in Him, why do I fail to get it right?
In Christ, I am told to write:
In Him, I do my best at night,
In Him, my life seems out of sight!

Of Christ, making my life the right;
Of Him, doing my all in all.
Of Him, listening to the altar call;
Of Christ, I'm endeavoring to run the race;
In Him, realizing, the gift to all.

At Christ, throwing my all in all,
In Him, giving up on self and selfishness,
And at Him, casting my very life enthralled—
To Christ, my Redeemer, Savior, I call,
To Him, my faith lifts me up with all!

To Christ alone, I gladly give my all!
To Him, I throw my guilt and fleece.
In Him, I find my perfect peace!
In Him alone, to conquer then recall
In Christ alone, I conquered then,—and now!

*(continued)*

*Brenda A. Kemper Purdy*

# In Christ Alone

In Christ, I find true, constant peace!
When all is yielded, then comes release!
Under Him as Lord, my pride will cease!
Under Him as Lord, my crown is sure!
Under Him, as Lord, I will endure!

Because—in Christ alone, I am secure!
And of Him— my task is sure.
Through Him, my guilt is absolved!
By Him, I'm wholly loved.
For Him, I will be moved!

When I'm leaning upon Christ and His Word!
Under Him, my victory *is* assured—
Now, **in** Him, I'm trusting in His Word.—
While in Him, it's plain to see
Nothing short of perfection through Christ, I'll be!

Christ in me, and I in Him!
In Christ alone,—is where I want to begin—
And in His Word, is where I read
Of Him, alone, taking o'er my heart!
And by Him, alone, getting me to start!

In Christ alone, throwing all of my heart—
To Him alone, yielding all that I start

*(continued)*

*Brenda A. Kemper Purdy*

## *OPENING MY HEART TO GOD*

For Him alone, that I choose to be part
Of Him alone, because I am choosing this way—
By Christ alone, I am living today!

In Christ, alone, I am perfecting my heart.
In Christ, alone does perfection exist!
In Christ, alone, I can truly, truly rest!
In Christ, alone, I am trusting the Best!
In Christ, alone, I am putting to the test. —

Of Him alone, as Christ's righteousness!
Of Him alone, in Christ's righteous Word.
In Him alone, **Victory** is assured!!!
By Him alone, you see 'tis true,
That in Christ, alone, is the state for you!

Of Him, in Whom, I have my trust—
In Him, alone, my duty—a must!
For in Christ, alone, is in Whom I dwell!
Therefore—by Him, in Him, through Him, the test
Of Christ alone, making sure, I'm at peace! —

While trusting, and obeying, whatever the test—
In Christ alone, I find perfect rest! —
Continuing in Him, for the rest of my life! —
Today in Him, I'll be without strife—

*(continued)*

*Brenda A. Kemper Purdy*

# In Christ Alone

In Christ alone, I pray, I will always be!

In Christ, in Christ, in Christ alone, you see—
In Him alone, to say and cry,
In Him alone, with all the praise that be,
By Christ alone, I yield to Thee—
In Christ alone, the Father to glorify!

Thank You Jesus, for what You've done!
Thank You Jesus, for the fact, You've won!
Thank You Jesus, that all this time—
You've been becoming, a Best Friend of mine!
Thank you God, that in Christ alone—

I rest my case—forever to be,
Sanctified totally— in Christ alone, you see!
To reach the glories of the Promised Land!
And with **Him**, alone,— I'll walk hand in hand—
Remembering the fact,— that—, **in Christ alone**, I stand!!

**The End!**

*Originally written early February 16, 2017, about 4:05 AM to 4:20 AM, and 11:40 to 11:55 AM, thinking I could go on and on! It was amended August 8, 2019; and completely finished about 12:35 PM on August 16, 2019.*

*Brenda A. Kemper Purdy*

# *Dear Lord, I So Long to Be Perfectly Whole*

*To be sung to the tune of Hymn# 318, "Whiter Than Snow," In the SDA Church Hymnal*

Dear Lord, I so long to be perfectly whole;
To sit at Your feet and be fully sold!
Sold out to You, Jesus, sold out to You, Lord;
Just make me Thy vessel, fully on board.

Refrain: The fullness of health with my body restored!
Now trusting Your promise, Lord—claiming Your Word!

It won't be long now that our Jesus will come
To take each person to their real home.
While I am waiting to see Your dear face—
May I experience Your full measure of grace!

Refrain: The fullness of health with my body restored!
Now trusting Your promise, Lord—claiming Your Word!

*(continued)*

*Brenda A. Kemper Purdy*

Dear Lord, I So Long to Be Perfectly Whole

> Grace to succeed and grace to overcome
> All of my faultiness so that I will know
> Beyond any shadows, beyond any care—
> That our parents and family will meet us there!!

Refrain: The fullness of health with our bodies restored!
Now trusting Your promise, Lord—claiming Your Word!

**The End!**

*Started Sabbath, September 9, 2017 about 4:30 AM. While I was waking up this Sabbath morning I began singing this tune and putting rhyming words to it; so I got up and prayed for God to give me words for a poem to this song. And He did! PTL!!! Amended at 7:30 AM same morning; also on Friday, July 19, 2019; and Friday, February 21, 2020.*

*Brenda A. Kemper Purdy*

# Today's Thoughts in Prayer

In this dark, dark world I pray,
Make me pure and clean today.
**Thank You for Your strength and power**
**To do Your will in this fine hour.**

Let me know the victory of success
In each eternal act and quest.
Please help me, Father, to obey
In all that You allow to come to me today.

Whate'er the task or plans I take,
May each be subject for me to make
Close contact to Your precious heart and side,
Where I have learned I may abide.

And reach into Your heart divine
To grasp totality sublime,
Of this day's duties performed so well
With perfect peace and then to tell—

To others how much *You* care
And how much *You* love me.
So that I will cast off this dark plight

*(continued)*

Brenda A. Kemper Purdy

Today's Thoughts in Prayer

### ***And shine for Jesus e'en through the night,***

That others will know I've been with You!
Today my prayer is that You'll see me through.
Walk closely, Jesus, in this heart of mine
That victory follows **Your** will divine!

### **Thank You for Your promises too,**
That tell the whole story of walking in You.
Let me begin today, I earnestly pray,—
To follow Your lead in what You say.

That makes life worth living the abundant way,
So that I'll experience peace, I pray, today!
Peace that surpasses all of my struggles of what to say
About my life in general and specific ways.

That I may perfectly reflect Your love
In a humble attitude given from above
Of perfect reliance upon Your strong arms
That enfold me with trust without any harm.

And the peace and joy that's only from above
Will carry me through this day with strength,
That I may experience Your forgiving, merciful**,**
### **LOVE—**

*(continued)*

*Brenda A. Kemper Purdy*

## OPENING MY HEART TO GOD

And show to the world there is victory from above!

**Thank You, Lord, for walking with me**
**And showing me *how* to gain VICTORY!**
That what I've begun with You in my heart,
You will finish in me right from the start!

That I will glorify You in all of my ways.
This is my heart's desire today—
That You will now go before me to guide my journey,
Forward to eternity and then some, I pray.

So please walk with me as You've promised!
**Thank You, Jesus,** for being with me this day!
**Thank You, Jesus,** for living in me—!
**Thank You,** for loving me so!!!

**Thank You, Jesus,** that *You* desire
Walking with me below in this very hour.
In this dark earth where *You* make light for the right!
**Thank *You*** for sharing *Your* strength and *Your* might!

**The End!**

*Begun as a prayer on Thursday, September 28, 2017,*
*about 6:50 AM, and finished approximately 7:30 AM;*
*amended Monday, October 2, 2019.*

Brenda A. Kemper Purdy

# *"Baby"*

Once upon a time—a six week young kitten arrived in
our home!
She was tiny and cute as can be—this Tabby kitten, you
see.
We named her "Baby" cause she fit into our hands
And would be like a baby daughter to us so grand!

Baby began her life with us away from her mommy
And continued to grow and romp each day—
She played with her toys much of the time—
Vigorously tumbling and rolling all around!

Baby is such a comical kitty to behold—
That we laugh and giggle time and time again—
When enjoying Baby's antics supremely!
In a God-given way, we could say.

We praise God, our Creator, for arranging this adoption,
And for the friend who gave her to us that day!!!
The friend was certain to find good homes
For Baby's brothers and sisters to roam.

She encouraged us to buy a cat tree

*(continued)*

*Brenda A. Kemper Purdy*

# OPENING MY HEART TO GOD

Which would help tame her seemingly unbounded energy—
So we did. And Baby loved it!—from day one with enthusiasm;
And proceeded growing freely more and more into the kitty she is today!

Anyone who loves cats will recognize for sure,
They are special, unique gifts from God!
Gentle giants, let's say.
That bless their owners every day

Showering love and support to help us endure—
Various hardships and daily tasks that we face
With loud, or soft, purring so gently and purely
While contentedly resting in our arms securely!

This contentment we must experience with Jesus—
Resting safely, firmly, yet gently in the Master's hands that carry us
Trusting our Maker to hold us close, near His heart and throne—
Just like Baby enjoys being near our very own!

She pours forth her adoration to us, her owners,
By purring so magnificently—

*(continued)*

"Baby"

That we feel the love and warmth shed abroad
From her life lived so abundantly!—

For Baby reflects God's way of dealing with His children;
How He gives us His love so graciously,
That one can not help but think
About God's love that is granted to each one daily!

All this because one kitty brings joy so vividly
Of the relationship it is our privilege to experience!
O what Love that would grant us such;
And relate to us His unconditional touch—

God certainly blesses us, through one of His creatures here below!
Just think about this the next time—
One caresses a kitten or animal so sublime.
**That God's creation helps to show us _more_ of His love so divine—**

Which **we can only begin to fathom** from above;
While trusting our Father in perfect **contentedness**—
Like Baby, if you will!—
Receiving God's love in spite of her mischievousness,

*(continued)*

*Brenda A. Kemper Purdy*

*OPENING MY HEART TO GOD*

And how He longs to tenderly embrace each one of us.
Just like we do to our "Baby"!
Who rests contentedly in our arms,
Giving us an abundance of love—because we first loved her completely—

Much like we are to respond to our Father in heaven,
Because He first loved us too—
And we are so very thankful for Baby!!!
**We must trust God** like our Baby does us!

He will never forget or abuse.
But instead, will tenderly care for, and assure us!
**As we tightly rest in God's arms by faith.**
**And like with Baby—accept His gracious goodness!**

**The End!**

*Started and finished on Wednesday, February 12, 2020 from 2-4 PM [PST]; It was amended Saturday night, February 15, 2020; Sunday, February 16, 2020; and Thursday, February 11, 2021. I spent a total of about 6 hours to completely finish.*

# My All for Jesus

What does this mean: "My All for Jesus"?
Am I totally surrendered to Him?
Jesus came to save me from sin.
Won't I please allow Him to come in?

Into my heart so dark and cold.
Into my goals and desires to be free.
Help me, Father, to totally yield up my life,
So that I may obtain sweet, sweet peace with Thee.

The kind of peace that passes knowledge
And passes understanding completely by.
I give You my heart, mind, body, and soul.
Please take full and complete control!

Somehow soothe the aching of my heart—
Help me, Jesus, to nevermore depart—
On old highways that would surely start
All the evil again that still plagues my heart.

Thank You, Jesus, that as I yield,
Three mighty forces come in to wield!
Whatever was wrong before is now right—

*(continued)*

*Brenda A. Kemper Purdy*

## *OPENING MY HEART TO GOD*

Because of a cleansing tide of pure white!

And Christ's blood now covers my soul
With power and strength to be had full well.
Victory in Jesus! Is now my motto;
Growing each day is my goal further—

*And my all for Jesus is now made new.—*
*My heart, mind, body, and soul.*
*Thank You, Lord, for making me whole!*
*Please, Lord, now forever, take full control!*

**The End!**

*I wrote this sometime between 2016 and 2018.*

# God Wins Out

In the middle of the night
As the darkness settles in—
**Remember—God wins out.**

When all I've done seems lost and wrong,
**Remember—He's in control of all!**

And when I think of what I can't do
Yet must in faith trust Him to see me through,
**Remember—God brings victory**
**In the way Jesus saves me.**

When much of my life flashes before me,
And I realize how He's led—
**Remember—I must trust Him now,**
**To bring me off more than conqueror instead!**

Not only in the world at large,
But in my personal life and character—
**I need remember—God knows best!!!**
**And will give me perfect rest!**

And as I sense my faltering steps on the road of life

*(continued)*

*Brenda A. Kemper Purdy*

## OPENING MY HEART TO GOD

Are part of the Master's test to win,
**I cast my helpless soul on Christ**
**Trusting fully to His merit alone!**


For God takes over now—
Since I've let Him fully lead.
And assurance comes as I draw my breath
To trust and follow Him indeed!


Please keep me close to Your heart, Oh God,
**As I learn to depend completely on Jesus.**
And cast my trembling weight on Him,
The One who makes my way perfect and joyous!


**Now—God sees me as the Redeemer does—**
A person willing to be made willing because
I sense the nearness of the Holy Spirit's presence
To comfort, bring peace, and leave me great assurance!


Please give me this peace, Oh Lord,
This kind that brings sweet release!
Praise You, Father, that in all this world of sin,
You are mighty to save and **conclusively *win*!**


**So remember—in the middle of the night—**
*I trust God to bring this transformation about.*

*(continued)*

*Brenda A. Kemper Purdy*

Now all should know that Jesus is my King,
**And God surely, truly, and completely—
Wins Out!!!**

**The End!**

*Written Sabbath, April 6, 2019, about 1:15 AM to 4:15 AM [PDT] by the Holy Spirit's inspiration; amended Wednesday, July 10, 2019 and Friday, July 26, 2019, [The Preparation Day for the Sabbath], finishing on Monday, July 29, 2019.*

*Brenda A. Kemper Purdy*

# *In Honor of My Beloved Husband, "Les"*

*Originally written Tuesday morning on August 6, 2019; amended Tuesday, August 13, 2019; and Tuesday evening, August 20, 2019; It took about five to seven hours to compose as I lovingly thought of my beloved Christian husband, and best earthly friend, other than Jesus, Leslie R. Purdy. (One can also replace the name "Les" with his/her spouse's name to personalize, and can shorten poem by choosing to read only after one or more pound [#] signs.)*

## #

"My heart is happy when I'm with you!
My heart is happy! No other one will do!
My heart is happy to be with you,
My heart is happy that you're so true!"

My Sweet~Sweet's happy, e'en though the way
Is oft so weary, let come what may!
For when I'm with him—he is so kind!
He walks alongside of me, even though I find

*(continued)*

Brenda A. Kemper Purdy

### In Honor of My Beloved Husband, "Les"

That troubles may come, as surely they do.
My heart is happy, that he fully trusts You!
Even in the daily grind, when all else is through.
My heart is happy, when he's so true!

Only by God's grace alone, we each will help
Each other home—, home to the kingdom—, the kingdom of love!
'Cause that's the result of trust placed in God!
Each sharing true happiness, as we walk along and plod

Our journey together, to the kingdom of God.
In all types of weather, come thunder, rain, or shine—
I'm happy that I am his,
And happy that he is mine!

Not just for today, but always
Throughout eternity divine!
Where we'll walk the heavenly land together
In which we'll loudly shout

The praises of our heavenly King!
That make huge hosannas ring!
And we'll walk together, hand in hand—
Along streets of gold—in the Promised Land!

*(continued)*

*Brenda A. Kemper Purdy*

# OPENING MY HEART TO GOD

### #

So I am content, and happy to be—
The wife of a wonderful, Christian man, you see!
And from here on out, I earnestly pray
I'll be worthy of the part to stay

Close beside this man of God today,
Because I am happy that he is mine,
And happy that I am his—to stay—
In loving relationship, forevermore, this day!

Praise God! Praise God! And praise God, again!
Amen. Amen. And amen to this end!
Thank You, Lord, for giving to me
The joy and happiness where we will come to be

Considered as one on this earth, as in days of yore,
When God created man, then Eve, before sin —
When this union between a man and a woman
Was certainly sacred, never to be broken!

### #

Thank you, Les, from the bottom of my heart.
Perseverance toward me in love,
Has won my affections, my heart, thereof—

*(continued)*

*Brenda A. Kemper Purdy*

In Honor of My Beloved Husband, "Les"

What God has said about a man and wife,

Let no man put asunder, whatever the strife!!
The tender ties that exist, between husband and wife
Are to help keep the family circle, close to the altar
With God as the center, so not one will falter.

I thank you, Sweetheart, for all you have been
And still are, so graciously following the Lord.
I'm perfectly happy to be by your side
As helpmeet and confidant to help stem the tide

In this world so full of sin,
Where happiness is hard to find—
Unless one is totally surrendered to Christ!!!
Let's make our days the happiest yet!!

For both of us to enjoy, and now to get
Our happiness, which depends on selfless love—
The kind that is enduring of all things, it seems,—
So that one can deny old selfish lusts,

And become victorious in Christ at last!
Thank you, Honey, for teaching me this—
To be selfless like Christ
Is where it's all at!

*(continued)*

*Brenda A. Kemper Purdy*

## OPENING MY HEART TO GOD

And one day soon, we will be able to say,
Oh God, we have waited for, this very *Day*!
And please take our hearts in Yours, God, today
To mold after the fashion of Your Word, we pray.

And make each of us truly, become perfect like You!
Because the reason we make it to Canaan Land thus,
Is strongly related to both our choices
Of becoming the man and woman God created us to be;

Not just now, but throughout all eternity!
So that I can truly say—
"My heart is happy when I'm with you, Les!
My heart is happy, Honey, because of you!

My heart is happy! No one else will do!
My heart is happy to become one with you!
And my heart is happy, that it's really true,
With Christ, all things are possible to thrive!

So my Honeybear, today,— please accept my offering
of praise, thanksgiving, and joy,
That you are the one God has chosen for me.
And let's walk hand in hand,
This path God has laid out now—, and then—,
throughout all eternity!"

**The End!**

*Brenda A. Kemper Purdy*

# I Surrender All

Dear Lord, I pray today
As I listen to Your voice anew,
I must die daily to self—
This I know I must do.

So, Lord, just now I surrender my all
To be made into Christ's likeness
With the character to not fall
Just for today into sin again.

That will mar my record and
Cause sadness to reign,
Not only in my heart
But in Jesus' heart too.

For He knows exactly
What I'm going through.
So now I must trust Him
Though scary it may be.

'Cause Jesus will grant to me
The strength that I need
To overcome self by His blood

*(continued)*

*Brenda A. Kemper Purdy*

## OPENING MY HEART TO GOD

So freely given to redeem man.

In cooperation with the Godhead
I am sure to more than win!
So keep me close to Your Spirit today, Lord.
Don't let me stray at all.

For I do not want to stumble again
And make such a terrible fall,
As yesterday. Please help me today, Lord—
I surrender all.

**The End!**

*Written sometime between 2017 and 2019, I believe.*

*Brenda A. Kemper Purdy*

*Brenda A. Kemper Purdy*

# God's Sleep Lullaby

*This lullaby is being sung by the Heavenly Father to His Only Begotten, Son, Jesus, when He would pray on the mountainside late in the evening and early morning hours.*

Sleep My Little One; sleep My Child.
I will take care of You because You are Mine.
Sleep. Sleep.—Sleep, right now;
You are My Precious One; so meek and mild.

Sleep now tho' stormy out, and all is so dark.
You will be safe with Me under the stars.
For I'm Your Shepherd dear, watching the night
So sleep, My Little One, You're in My sight.

Sleep, Little One. Sleep right now.
Close Your eyes so tight; then somehow
I will make of You all the night long
Just what You want Me to, and all the day through.

Night comes before daybreak when I will do
Just what You want Me to, all the day through.
So sleep, My Little One; sleep, My Child—
Precious is the sight of My Perfect Child's view!

*(continued)*

*Brenda A. Kemper Purdy*

## OPENING MY HEART TO GOD

Sleep. Sleep—sleep right now.
I will take care of You; trust Me tonight.
So I will make of You perfect and right
Just what You want of Me—in this dark night.

Sleep. Sleep. Trust My Word
So You can grow up to be just like Your God!
Gently now, — simply trust in Me
As I restore Your strength and destiny.

Now wait till I call You
Out of the night.
Place all of Your trust in Me,
And You will be righteous!

So sleep and trust in Me—to do what You can not.
Rest now, My Little One,— the day will come
When You will wake refreshed, ready to serve
Faithfully, in the vineyard of the Lord.

Sweet dreams, My Precious One, soon look to the day
When You will rise to sing—praises to Your King!
Sleep on now to dream—of trusting Me as God!
You are My Begotten,— soon walk with Me, Son!

Just rest now until—morning's begun.

*(continued)*

So sweet is Your sleep to Me, My Precious Child!
You are the embodiment, of all hope and love!
So I will bless You now—to bask in My love!

### **The End!**

*I began writing this perhaps in 2009. However, I finished it on Friday, August 16, 2019.*

# Just for Today

*I woke up with these words on my mind, "Just for today—, Make me like You…", so I got up for devotions and wrote. It took about two hours to compose, and I started about 4 AM on August 23, 2019.*
*To God be the glory!*

**Just for today—**
**Make me like You.**
Help me, Lord,
To really subdue
My heart and feelings
That I may know
What You expect of me
Down here below!

And as I awake
To place my trust
Completely, solely in You—
May I cause heaven
To sing and rejoice!
That my life in this morning
Will awaken with *choice*—
To serve You freely

*(continued)*

Brenda A. Kemper Purdy

# Just for Today

In whatever I do—
**Just for today.**

That I may become
Fully surrendered—
Growing more and more,
Listening to Your voice
And walking here below,
Just exactly—
*Where You want me to go!*
**Just for today—**
Make me completely like You!

And then when my case
Comes up in the courts above,
May I trust in Your *VICTORY*
You've given so much of,
To this lowly servant of yours.
And then—
Trust in you always
For every moment of livin'
**Just for today—**
*For that's all that I'm given!*

**Just for today, just for today—**
My Lord and I

*(continued)*

*Brenda A. Kemper Purdy*

## *OPENING MY HEART TO GOD*

Trusting I pray.
So now as I begin my day—
I'll go about living
Like *You*, I pray!
**Just for today.**

**PTL!!!**

**The End!**

# Empathy

Such a sensitive soul as *You, O Christ*
It would really be nice to know—
If You had troubles just like I?—

But in *Your Word*, You tell us so—
I need just believe, no matter the cost
That God went to the cross so I might not be lost!

And now I search where it is found
That I need surrender all to One
Who loved me, and gave me **His** crown!—

Sometimes it's difficult to see
*That all the while I'm searching for Him*
*He's coming after me!*

**The End!**

*Composed on August 28, 2019, about 8:30 in the morning.*

*Brenda A. Kemper Purdy*

# God's Math...

## Husband and Wife

Or
*(Les) and (Brenda)*

## *Jesus*

---

## = True Joy

### & A Happy Home!!!
PTL!!!

*(May substitute name with one's own)*
*Drawn August 28, 2019.*

*Brenda A. Kemper Purdy*

# *Expectations*

***For A Happy Eden Home—Bren's Practical Advice for Spouses started years ago; finished August 29, 2019.***

**The Explanation of the Following Principle: That—**

Someone else may be more **attractive aesthetically** to you, but that same person is not as **appealing aesthetically** to you as the one you've chosen to love. <u>***The physical attraction of someone else is only momentary.***</u>

<u>***The physical appeal and attraction of the one you love is abiding and constant.***</u>

There **should be no physical attraction of someone else that is more than momentary**, *as it could lead to lusting.* **Physical Attraction or Physical Appeal involves Choice.**

**Again:**

**A. Attraction aesthetically** = *meaning outward appearance and form that catches your eye as pleasing =* **Momentary Attraction.**

**B. Appealing aesthetically** = *meaning outward appearance and form that you choose to appreciate and enjoy*

*(continued)*

*for its unique beauty.* (It may or may not catch your eye as pleasing at first.) It is ***lasting.***

**A. This involves a goodwill attitude of Christian love toward** *all* **of God's created individual beings.**

**B. This involves choosing only** *one* **of these created individual beings as your help meet** *and loving that one being totally and completely, thinking and believing the one you're committed to is the most beautiful in each and every way to you—because God made him (or her) especially for* ***you!***

**Remember:**

**Physical Attraction lasts only a moment.** <u>**Character is what really makes a person beautiful or handsome. Character endures. It IS the appeal.**</u> *The Bible says, "Favour is deceitful, and beauty is vain: but a woman that feareth the L*ORD*, she shall be praised." (Proverbs 31:30); "How fair and how pleasant art thou, O love, for delights!" (Song of Solomon 7:6); "O my dove, … for sweet is thy voice, and thy countenance is comely" (Song of Solomon 2:14); "My beloved is mine, and I am his" (Song of Solomon 2:16).* <u>***These principles will bring BALANCE to the equation.***</u>

**The End.**

# A Motto

**If you want God to be there and the gospel to be real in your life—**

**You must:**

**Want to *live it*—**
***Believe it*—**
**And *give it!***

**The End!**

*I wrote this sometime between the years 2000 and 2017, I believe. And I amended it in 2019, and February 4, 2020.*

*Brenda A. Kemper Purdy*

# *My Heartfelt Plea—*

### *I Cry:*
O Lord I need help!
I'm sick. I feel bad. Crushing, and like I'm vomiting all over You, God.
I need Your robe of white righteousness—
*To cover me!*

Please help me now, O God, some way.
I surely do need a clean slate today!
A transformation I would say—
Nothing short of a heart transplant to stay!

## GOD SAYS:

On top of the problems for the current time,
I'll be with you and guide you, if you'll let Me preside
In the throne room right where—
Your choice and decision-making hide.

Where black is black and red is red.
I'll give you the power to turn the tide,
Into turbo-making energy that produces quite well

*(continued)*

*OPENING MY HEART TO GOD*

All the tasks that I've asked you to show Me until—

The great, great, Day of My Soon Coming, My child!
**That** will be—
***When all will be rectified!***
***Yes, even your words.***

# I RESPOND:

Thank You, Lord, for listening to me—for You to cover me in a robe of pure white!
***This is truly, my heartfelt plea!***
***And as I go through this day, please walk right beside me—***
***And carry me along with Your Holy Spirit to guide me!***

**The End!**

*Inspired by verses in James 4:13 and onward. This was composed sometime in the past twenty years, and was amended on September 9, 2019; February 4, 2020; and finally on Wednesday, June 17, 2020.*

Brenda A. Kemper Purdy

# TRUST ME

*As I ponder today how my life has been thus far—*
*I wonder deep inside, am I right with God?*
*Do I have the anointing of the Spirit*
*To do God's Word, not just hear it?*

*The impression comes that I do love Jesus,*
*And walk with Him daily; but there's more—*
*Jesus says to "trust me completely*
*E'en though the way may be sore."*

*How, may I ask, do I do that, my Lord?*
***"By claiming the promises that are in My Word!***
***Believe in Me, and you will be saved!***
***Trust Me** and follow e'en though it's not paved.*

*"For my way is always the "narrow" way, you see*
*And you must give me your will right now—*
*So humble yourself and cast all upon me,*
*The burdens or trials that you bare each day.*

*"And I will make of you something lasting and beautiful*
*By purging your sins, if you will let Me in!*
*But in order for Me to make this to happen—*

*(continued)*

Brenda A. Kemper Purdy

## *OPENING MY HEART TO GOD*

*You must <u>trust Me!</u>*

*"**Trust Me** when I say that I love you*
*More than you ever can certainly know!*
***Trust Me** to do what you can not do.*
***Trust Me** to help you **grow!!!***

*"**Trust Me** when the way may get frightful;*
***Trust Me** whene'er your feeling doubtful;*
***Trust Me to take away all of your fears***
*And make you brave in the face of certain tears.*

*"**Trust Me that I will actually finish***
*What I started in you long ago.*
***Trust Me** that I will recreate, and make your soul*
*perfect*
*In the grace that I give to you just now.*

*"And as you learn to **trust Me***
*With all your heart, mind, body, and soul—*
*Please notice that **I am coming <u>with</u> you***
*<u>**Walking right beside you too.**</u>"*

*So just now before I retire,*
*As I hear your voice speak to my heart and mind,*
***Help me, Lord,** <u>not trust my feelings</u>*

*(continued)*

Brenda A. Kemper Purdy

TRUST ME

<u>*But trust You fully*</u> *that I may find*

*Myself doing what You desire only,*
*Not my will—but Thine—*
<u>*Not just for a moment,*</u>
<u>*But for all the moments—down through the corridors*</u>
<u>*of time!*</u>

**THE END!**

*Written Sunday, February 16, 2020, before retiring for the night; amended slightly, Monday, February 17, 2020.*

*Brenda A. Kemper Purdy*

# *If I*

***If I*** "hit the bed" now, Lord—
I may sleep, but—I certainly will remember and peep—
the fact that You're the One who gives the orders!
So—let's hear it for this turn of events.

Then I know that Jesus will be my partner too,
To take on the world so deep and blue!
But wait, oh God—what do **You** want?
Do You really, really want **my** personal thoughts??

They are so finite here below!
It seems they are just so tense—You know?
That I can't place the light I last saw, 'tis true.
So much needs to be done for me by **You!**

Your hands, Your feet, Your loving touches, Lord,
Through modern miracles left and right,
Are causing me to say to **You** tonight,
Please, oh God, ***if I*** can pray—**please,**
Keep all my evil thoughts away!
And promise I'll someday become

Whole, complete, like **You** want me to be!
Where nothing matters but character, You see—

*(continued)*

*Brenda A. Kemper Purdy*

If I

And fully consecrated destinies!
What's that I hear, dear Lord, just now?

A still, small voice saying then and now—
That all I need is to stop long enough,
To place my hand and heart inside this house
Into Your big hands and heart somehow,

To go where You want me to go just now!
Humbly, meekly, **please,**— Lord!
I accept Your challenge to trust in **You.**
When *if I* can but yield my sin-stained life

To Your complete will,
For the fulfillment of my life,
*I will. I do. In the quiet of this moment.*
Please help me, God, to list' to Your yearning

Of where You want me to serve You most—
Whether far, or near, or somewhere close!
And *if I* abide in **You**, and **You** abide in *me—*
*I will follow You—through all eternity!*

**The End!**

*Written about 3:20 AM on March 13, 2012; slightly amended on Thursday, June 18, 2020, and September 8, 2020.*

*Brenda A. Kemper Purdy*

# Start. Stop. Look Up and Live!

**Jesus does never condemn.**
**You may feel lost, but—,**
**Hope is not gone!**
**He's always near your heart!**

*Look up and live!*

Just stop to listen to His voice!
You'll find He's always there—
Suggesting left. Suggesting right.
Suggesting how to live.

*Look up and live!*

So if you want to go to heaven,
Use your faith and find
All you need is to start and feel
His arms around you then.

*For you must start; then stop to look up!*
*Look up and you will live!*

*(continued)*

*Brenda A. Kemper Purdy*

And when you get discouraged,
"I'll be there with you," He said.
"Don't give up on the good ship, Zion
For I will see her come to port in time.

**"And you will rally too!"**
God is **victorious**! God is **victorious**!
He is **victorious** for you and me!
Whenever you need Him—He's always there.

*Just look up and live!*

Christ will set you free.
Do you want Him to do this?
All He needs is you!
So—
**Start. Stop. Look up and live!**

*It's a plain necessity—*
*To always keep your focus lifted*
*To the One Who can set you free.*

**The End!**

*(continued)*

Start. Stop. Look Up and Live!

*I don't recall when I wrote this, but I added to it a lot on Monday, September 9, 2019. It was amended again on Sunday, February 23, 2020.*

\*\*\*

May each of you have been richly blessed by reading this volume of devotional prayers in poetry and prose, and drawn much closer to Jesus in your own walk with the Lord! This is my prayer!!

*—The author*

## TEACH Services, Inc.
P U B L I S H I N G

We invite you to view the complete
selection of titles we publish at:
**www.TEACHServices.com**


We encourage you to write us
with your thoughts about this,
or any other book we publish at:
**info@TEACHServices.com**


TEACH Services' titles may be purchased in
bulk quantities for educational, fund-raising,
business, or promotional use.
**bulksales@TEACHServices.com**


Finally, if you are interested in seeing
your own book in print, please contact us at:
**publishing@TEACHServices.com**

We are happy to review your manuscript at no charge.